This is a biography of a hero of the AIDS pandemic as told by a mother.

Tony Carden worked with civil society to share his experiences, living with HIV. He helped educate directors, dentists and school children. He survived child abuse, discrimination and grief to spread the message of love and knowledge. He was a force for good. And so is his mother Lesley who tells her son's story with loyalty and pride.

This is a book about a struggle against AIDS at a time when it was usually unsuccessful.

With a brilliant career as an actor behind him, Tony Carden suddenly found himself performing on a stage of tears.

His work with ACON to support those newly diagnosed with HIV/AIDS, and spreading the safe sex message to hundreds of secondary school students throughout Sydney is uplifting and reassuring.

His diary entries, now presented in this book, reveal a deep soul who turned misfortune into liberation.

The Hon. Justice Michael Kirby AC CMG

* * *

I knew Tony as an activist and a friend. We started working together in 1991 to get desperately needed funding for Ward 17 South, the AIDS ward at Sydney's St Vincent's Hospital. While I worked at the parliamentary level, Tony worked with the AIDS activist group ACT UP to raise public awareness with imaginative and challenging grassroots action.

While he could be demanding and outrageous, he was the most appreciative and supportive person, even when he was dealing with the severe impact of HIV.

One of my most moving memories of Tony is the 1994 Sydney Gay and Lesbian Mardi Gras when he organised a group of gay and straight, short and tall, moustached, bearded and clean shaven men and women to take part in the Parade as 'The Clovers'.

Lesley gives the background to that event, a story which illustrates Tony's imagination, organisational skills and guile! There are many such stories throughout the book.

In telling Tony's life story, *I Don't Want to Talk About It* also reminds us of a challenging period in our most recent history, particularly for the LGBTQIA+ community and shows us that determination and courage will triumph. It also ensures that Tony's significant contribution to the fight against AIDS will not be forgotten.
Sydney Lord Mayor – Councillor Clover Moore AO

* * *

This book highlights the pain and courage of victims of childhood abuse. I believe this book about Tony's life will help many people who have been through similar experiences, as well as their loved ones.
Peter Andrew Karp, Senior Partner, Karp O'Neill Lawyers, 2022

* * *

Tony's intuitiveness and creativity were balanced by a strong and forceful personality. What else are activists made of?
Michael Glynn, Founder and Editor, *Sydney Star Observer*, **1995 (deceased)**

* * *

I wish I had known him. I envy those who did. He was a warrior for our times – an actor turned activist who used his creativity and forceful personality to help change the lives of people living with AIDS. He was a gentle and loving, unpredictable, sometimes outrageous young man with the courage of his convictions and an ability to ACT UP.
Tony Begbie, Journalist, UK and Australia, 1996

* * *

Extremely funny, extremely outrageous, to the point of us thinking: *He's going to get himself arrested.* Tony was very wilful – he'd play little tricks ...
Kirsty Machon, Research Scientist, Fellow Activist, 1995

* * *

Tony Carden was an artist and the role of an artist is to speak out for political freedom.
Sydney Star Observer, **Obituaries, September 1995**

* * *

Warrior Blood is more an activist's statement than an artwork.
Talkabout Magazine, **October 1994**

* * *

On behalf of the ACT Place Names Advisory Committee, I am pleased to confirm the approval of the public place name **Carden Street** in the ACT division (suburb) of Denman Prospect. The new place name commemorates your son, Mr Anthony (Tony) Carden, for his contributions as an advocate and activist for people living with Acquired Immune Deficiency Syndrome (AIDS) and the human immunodeficiency virus and to social reform.

* * *

I Don't Want to Talk About It

A biography of AIDS warrior Tony Carden

Lesley Saddington

*For the warriors, for those they fought for,
and for Tony,
who was valiant 'gainst all disaster'*

Some names and identifying details have been changed or redacted to protect the privacy of individuals and institutions.

First published in 2024 by Lesley Saddington

© Lesley Saddington 2024
The moral rights of the author have been asserted

All rights reserved. Except as permitted under the *Australian Copyright Act 1968* (for example, a fair dealing for the purposes of study, research, criticism or review), no part of this book may be reproduced, stored in a retrieval system, communicated or transmitted in any form or by any means without prior written permission.

All inquiries should be made to the author.

"Nonno's Poem" from *Night of the Iguana* by Tennessee Williams. Copyright © 1960, 1972 by The University of the South. Reprinted by permission of Georges Borchardt, Inc. on behalf of the University of the South. All rights reserved.

A catalogue entry for this book is available from the National Library of Australia.

ISBN: 978-1-923007-96-3

Printed in Australia by Pegasus
Book production and text design by Publish Central
Cover design by Julia Kuris
Back cover photograph courtesy of Jamie Dunbar www.jamiedunbar.com.

The paper this book is printed on is certified as environmentally friendly.

Contents

Prologue	xi

Part One Legacy of a Warrior

Chapter 1	The Tainted Saint	3
Chapter 2	An Unfinished Memoir	6

Part Two The Making of a Warrior

Chapter 3	Tony-ony-Macaroni	13
Chapter 4	Tone	18
Chapter 5	'It'	24
Chapter 6	Escape	33
Chapter 7	Betrayed	44
Chapter 8	The Blue Suitcase	53
Chapter 9	Children and Art	67
Chapter 10	Call to Arms	84
Chapter 11	'I Don't Want to Talk About It'	96
Chapter 12	Purple Presage	108

Part Three The War

Chapter 13	Light on the Shore	118
Chapter 14	Buyers Club	128
Chapter 15	No Room at the Inn	137
Chapter 16	'Take No Bullshit'	144
Chapter 17	Caught!	158
Chapter 18	One Hundred Beds and 907 White Carnations	166
Chapter 19	Someone's Uncle	175
Chapter 20	The Bill	183
Chapter 21	Mardi Gras and The Twenty Clovers	192
Chapter 22	'Only a Pinprick'	202
Chapter 23	The Orange Branch	210
Chapter 24	Freesias	223

Part Four Requiem

Chapter 25	Final Bow	234
Chapter 26	Return of the Warriors	238
Chapter 27	Pilgrimage	253

Epilogue	258
Bibliography	270
Acknowledgements	272
About the Author	276

Prologue

The trust of a child is a sacred privilege. Those who betray that trust destroy childhood's innocence and cast shadows over the life that lies ahead.

My son Tony Carden was 33 years old when he died of AIDS (Acquired Immune Deficiency Syndrome). From the moment I held him as a newborn and looked into his soulful brown eyes I sensed he had a unique destiny. I watched him negotiate the challenges of childhood but knew little of his private battles. I cheered as his creative career as an actor soared, and marvelled at his wit, resourcefulness and resilience, his warrior energy.

Even after he was diagnosed with AIDS, in the midst of his own struggles, he fought for the rights of others living with the disease as they endured vilification and public hatred.

It was my role as a witness to the courageous way he dealt with his childhood torment, his ravaging illness and the appalling discrimination he suffered as a gay man – both in life and death – that changed me forever.

For a long time after Tony died, I closed my door on a brutal world. In this brave new landscape, this scattered universe, I gradually rediscovered my son and came to know him in a different way: through his private letters, through the eyes of his dearest friends and from the memories of his much-loved 'other family'. I wept and raged when I discovered the ugly truth behind his childhood secret. In doing so, I renewed my courage to fight on his behalf for everything he believed in.

Part 1

Legacy of a Warrior

Chapter 1

The Tainted Saint

2002

'Hello, is this Lesley Saddington, mother of Tony Carden?'

Hearing his name jolted me, a painful reminder that he'd been dead for seven years.

'You may remember me, Lesley. I'm Justin Chase,[1] the manager of Ward 17 South at St Vincent's Hospital. I'm calling about the painting *Acacius (Stigmata)*.'

I did remember Justin, and my mind flew back to the day we'd met, in 1996, when the portrait of Tony was hung in Ward 17 South.

Sydney's leading AIDS ward, once inadequate and ill-equipped to deal with the HIV epidemic, had undergone a million-dollar renovation, and Tony was one of the main drivers behind the campaign. I remembered the painting. Artist AñA Wojak had created a stunning portrait of Tony as Saint Acacius, patron saint of martyrs in traditional icon style.

AñA had salvaged a weathered cedar door for the portrait's canvas. The 23-carat gold leaf applied as the background caressed and shadowed the flaws and grain of the old wood, and the vibrant blue of lapis lazuli outlined the frame and Tony's white robe. He was posed with care, with his figure erect, his blond hair brushed simply

---

1 Pseudonym.

to one side, arms loose, fingers elegantly lifted, a stigmata scar on his forehead, a gleaming halo of gold symbolising his sainthood. His gaze was level and direct, his eyes sad yet somehow challenging.

I wondered whether the painting had been damaged, perhaps stolen, but what came next made little sense.

'The hospital board has decided to return the painting to you,' Justin said. 'We'd like you to come and collect it as soon as you can. Just let me know when you'll be here, and I'll arrange to have someone to carry it out for you.'

'I beg your pardon, Justin? I'm not sure I understand. *Acacius (Stigmata)* belongs to St Vincent's. Surely you remember. Why would they decide to return it?' I implored.

Justin had been there that autumn morning when the portrait had been presented to the hospital to hang in the AIDS ward. It was a festive occasion, with VIPs, local MP Clover Moore, the hospital's superintendent, AñA and people from the gay community[2] were present. There'd been a photo and write-up of the presentation ceremony in the following day's *Sydney Morning Herald*.

Justin hesitated and sighed. 'Look, I'm sorry, Lesley, but a couple of members of the board have decided it's inappropriate for a gay man to be portrayed as a Catholic saint.'

So that was it – the old bogey of discrimination, rearing its ugly head yet again. Society's mistreatment of its most vulnerable had needled Tony since his childhood trauma. Even now, after death, it taunted him. Justin would have known that the money to renovate the ward had been raised largely due to the unflagging efforts of the gay man depicted in the painting. Yes, the artist had represented Tony as a saint, and why not? He was the very stuff martyrs are made of. I knew of no better Earthly representation Saint Acacius could have had than as a courageous young man, gay or otherwise, sacrificing himself for others. I ached for him.

---

2   Today referred to as the LGBTQI+ community.

'The board's membership changes from time to time,' Justin explained. 'We have a couple of new members, so that's probably why they've arrived at this decision. It's disappointing, I agree, but I've simply been instructed to make the arrangements.'

I realised that Justin, who'd cared so compassionately for Ward 17 South's patients, had been put in the hot seat. He was yet another victim of bigotry, so why take out my anger on him?

The following day I emptied the boot of my car, lined it with blankets and drove to St Vincent's. Still smarting with anger and humiliation, I took the lift to Ward 17 South, and there in the space where *Acacius (Stigmata)* had hung was a wishy-washy watercolour of a serene field of flowers, uninspiring and unlikely to stir religious resentment.

Justin greeted me with an awkward smile. 'Would you mind parking down the side of the hospital? Then we can carry the painting out through the side door directly to your car.'

Borne triumphantly through the main entrance six years earlier, *Acacius (Stigmata)* was to be sneaked through a side door as though in disgrace. Two white-gowned orderlies carried the painting, wrapped in a white cotton hospital-issue blanket, to my car. Overwhelmed by humiliation and hurt, I barely noticed the bustling city passing by as I drove towards the tranquillity of my bushland home where *Acacius (Stigmata)* would find safe refuge.

I manoeuvred the portrait inch by inch through the carport and into the house. Tenderly I set it against the living-room wall. Tony's eyes looked pensive, as though reflecting on the way his life had unfolded. I'd never expected to become the portrait's custodian but I knew its journey could not end here, not like this. I didn't yet know how far *Acacius (Stigmata)* and I would need to travel to find its final resting place.

Chapter 2

The Unfinished Memoir

Tony met Sydney artist AñA Wojak in 1991 at a Sydney meeting of AIDS Coalition to Unleash Power (ACT UP). AñA was working towards an exhibition called 'Stigmata', comprising portraits of martyrs from Mary Magdalene to Joan of Arc. AñA was impressed by Tony's fierce determination to improve the lives of others, but suspected that his jovial wit was masking his suffering.

Believing him to be a martyr of the AIDS epidemic, fighting for the rights of others while suffering himself, AñA had decided that Tony was ideally suited to portray Saint Acacius.

Religious mythology tells that Acacius led thousands of Roman soldiers into battle to defend their religious beliefs. When the Christian warriors among them were to be crucified for refusing to denounce their faith, Acacius prayed to God that as a reward for their loyalty, his followers would be restored in body and mind. This concept of healing appealed to AñA, whose fervent wish was that those with AIDS might be similarly blessed. AñA asked Tony to model for the painting of Saint Acacius and Tony agreed.

1995

AñA contacted me a few days before Tony's funeral. 'I think it would be appropriate to have *Acacius (Stigmata)* on display at the wake because it would mean a great deal to the gay community.'

Acacius (Stigmata) was on display in a Paddington gallery, and I'd intended to pay it a visit soon. AñA's perception was astute: having it at Tony's wake would mean that both Tony's 'families' would have the opportunity to appreciate it.

Grateful for such thoughtfulness, I agreed and said that the wake would be held at a gallery in Glebe, the home of Roy, my 'Ankali', and his partner, Jim.

Several months earlier, as Tony's health had declined and his need for support increased, Alan, an ACON (AIDS Council of NSW) volunteer, contacted me to tell me about the Ankali Project, a service that provides volunteers trained by the East Sydney Area Health Service as one-on-one support to AIDS patients and/or their next of kin. He suggested that an Ankali (the Koorie word for 'friend') might be helpful for both Tony and me. Tony politely declined but to me, it was like being offered a friendly hand to ease the way across increasingly rocky terrain. I bonded easily with Roy, a university lecturer in nursing, and he became my main support over the next five months. We would meet every week, perhaps for lunch, a ferry ride or a stroll in the park, for some laughter, an occasional tear. He provided me rare empathy for my aching heart. Roy generously offered his home in which to hold Tony's wake.

Bow-tied waiters bustled among groups of mourners, serving champagne to a throng of almost five hundred as they streamed into Gallery 483. The gallery's exhibition 'Human Figure Sketches and Paintings' provided the ideal backdrop for *Acacius (Stigmata)*, which had pride of place on a large wooden easel.

Whispered suggestions to the effect that it should be hanging at St Vincent's in Ward 17 South were followed by nodding heads and murmurs of 'Yes, that's definitely where it belongs'. Eventually the ripples became a wave of resolution: 'We have to find a way to buy it and have it hung in the AIDS ward in memory of Tony and ACT UP.'

Sensing they awaited an initiative, I stood beside the portrait and announced, 'I'll put down $1000 to get things started. Let's see where we can go from there.'

Elizabeth Morson, who had also lost her son to AIDS, added another thousand and by the end of the afternoon, AñA accepted the sum we'd raised.

A day that had begun with an outpouring of grief ended with a sense of achievement.

* * *

Two weeks later, with heavy heart, I sat in Tony's deserted flat to work my way through his belongings before returning his key to public housing. As I sorted his meagre possessions, mostly books, records and audio tapes, I put aside anything I thought a particular friend or family member might appreciate.

Warrior Blood, the acclaimed artwork Tony had created in 1991 for a National Gallery exhibition stood proudly displayed atop his

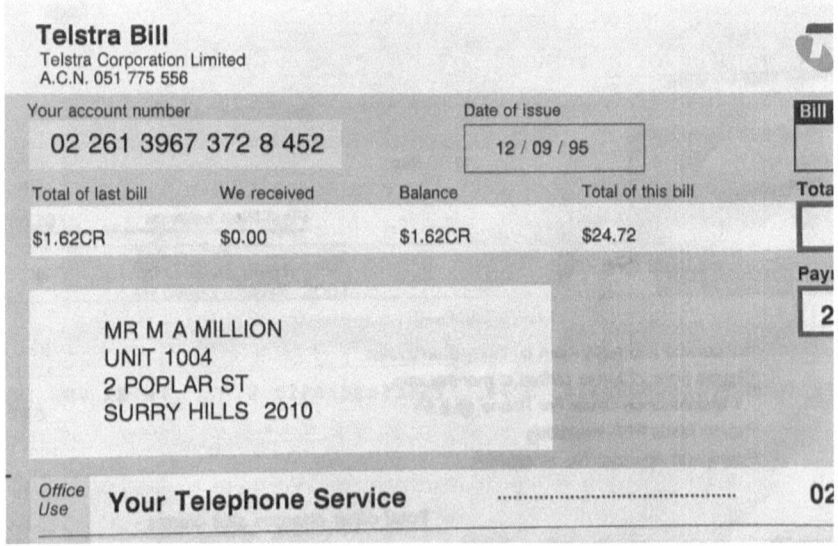

Telephone bill for Tony's alias 'Mr M A Million', when he was struggling to make ends meet, 1995.

bookshelf, radiating its message of hope: that there would be more warriors to continue the battle against AIDS after he was gone . . . I studied it and sighed. *Warrior Blood* would have to come home with me until I could find a more appropriate place for it.

On the covers of several books and video tapes were affixed a red heart sticker. These I put aside in a separate pile, uncertain of the stickers' significance until I discovered a blue writing pad in the bottom of his wardrobe, tucked away in a cardboard box with a matching red-heart sticker clearly displayed on top. I lifted the pad's cover and found to my great delight that he'd written on several pages, in a shakier hand than his once boldly flourished script. He'd titled the pages, 'Essays from a Victim – An AIDS Story'. It seemed to be the beginning of what he'd intended to become his autobiography, but he'd managed only twelve pages. He'd left it too late.

One day, when the time is right, I thought, *I'll write your story for you* . . .

Part 2
The Making of a Warrior

The report of the Commonwealth Film Censorship Board, issued recently, has just come to our notice. The Board reports that films are becoming 'more mature' in their themes, and says that they dealt with subjects which, by their nature, were designed to shock such as rape, nymphomania, homosexuality, prostitution, abortion, drug addiction and delinquency.

The Tribune, October 1961

Chapter 3

Tony-ony-Macaroni

1961

It was a perfect Sydney summer's day: cicadas were shrilling in the treetops, gardens garlanded with blue agapanthus and scarlet Christmas bush were joyously heralding the arrival of new life. Our son, Anthony Charles, had been born during the night after a three-day labour and I was resting. He'd beaten Santa by three days so to his siblings he was an early present, a living toy. Four-year-old Jane stuffed his mouth with a welcoming slice of Christmas cake and two-year-old Phil lovingly placed a collection of splintery sticks into his new brother's crib.

It was only in the early mornings while the rest of household slept that I had him to myself. I'd cradle the warm bundle in my arms, take his tiny hand in mine and marvel at his long fingers, so unlike the broad, practical hands of his father and brother. I was optimistic that my hope for my children to have a brother and a sister each was looking like being fulfilled. Jane and Philip now had their brother. Three years later the plan would reach fruition with the arrival of Carolyn, who would swell the trio to a quartet. In the Aussie custom of shortening names, 'Philip' became 'Phil', 'Anthony' became 'Tony', and 'Carolyn', a three-syllable tongue-twister for tiny tongues, became 'Lynna'. 'Jane', of course, remained 'Jane'.

I had grown up in a family beholden to the demands of Victorian-era discipline a confidence-sapping experience I was determined not to inflict on the next generation. My hopes for a university education had been passed off as a waste of time and money, essential for sons but not for daughters, who would ultimately marry and find fulfilment in motherhood.

Rebellion was out of the question, so if marriage and motherhood were to be my career, I'd do it in spades. Mine would be a 'yes' home, not a 'no' home like the one I'd grown up in, where disapproval outweighed approval, and it would have stability, unlike the unsettling succession of houses and schools that had been the lot of my brother and me as the children of a schoolteacher who was regularly promoted to a new school.

When I was fourteen and my high school end-of-year dance was looming, we students were instructed by the teachers to invite a partner. Invite a boy? Me? *Quelle horreur!* Dreading rejection, and keeping my head lowered to hide my reddening cheeks, I invited Keith Carden, an outgoing sixteen-year-old I'd met at the local church fellowship, to be my partner. He agreed, despite being warned by the fellowship's leader 'You'll be dancing your way to Hell, lad.'

Stocky and jolly, Keith had a robust lust for life and a raunchy sense of humour that were a refreshing change from the strait-laced upbringing I'd known. His ready smile and easygoing manner were reassuring, infectious. Working outdoors had bronzed his muscular arms and legs and bleached his hair but even the Australian sun couldn't bleach his distinctive black eyebrows, which our sons would one day inherit.

Five years later, in 1956, when I was nineteen and Keith twenty-two, we married in the church where we'd met. Everyone approved and, as was the custom of the day, I promised in my marriage vows to obey.

The Cardens had been builders in Sydney for more than a century following the arrival in 1844 from England of two Carden brothers, who were commissioned to build an ornate spiral staircase in Customs House at Circular Quay. Keith was the first of the family's fifth generation to follow suit. We took the plunge and registered our own building partnership, Carden Constructions. We'd build 'spec' houses: family homes with versatile designs on premium blocks of land, the 'speculation' component being whether or not we'd be able to maintain cashflow by achieving fast, profitable sales.

We worked and saved, and when Jane arrived a year later, I quickly learnt the art of multi-tasking. I combined motherhood with part-time work and thrifty budgeting until we were eventually able to afford a block of land in an outlying Sydney suburb.

With the naïve confidence of young beginners and with a courageous 'no hide, no Christmas box' optimism, we visited the rotund, waistcoated bank manager Mr Draper to apply for a building overdraft. An unexpected twinkle in his eye as he shook Keith's hand inspired optimism. He listed our modest assets, added a couple of hypothetical extras, leant back in his chair and beamed. 'This looks pretty good, you know, and if the worst happens and the house doesn't sell, you'll just have to move into it yourselves and start paying off a mortgage. How's that?'

We left his office on a cloud of dream-houses.

Keith multi-tasked as builder, carpenter–joiner and labourer while I organised sub-contractors, and cleaned bricks, floors and windows and gathered anything that happened managed to fall from tradesmen's barrows. We learnt everything the hard way: negotiating with sub-contractors, dealing with devious real estate agents, steering potential sales to fruition, liaising with solicitors, the water board and local councils, and, most challenging of all for raw young beginners, presenting as polished professionals to our clients, who were often of our parents' generation. We did as much as we could do ourselves. Jane, at eighteen months old, gurgled and played in her Moses basket beside me as I wiped paint from my arms and legs and vowed I'd never paint another picket fence.

Within two years we'd built and sold four spec houses and were sufficiently solvent to make a small, white-painted, colonial-style house our heavily mortgaged home, just in time for the arrival of Phil.

Keith was soon building a succession of houses, both spec and contract, and I was not only housewife and mother of two but secretary and business partner as well. Although I did my best to adapt to the routine of the building industry's 'early to bed and early to rise' lifestyle, understanding their 'weird mob' jargon was another.

I seldom saw bed before midnight, but I enjoyed every moment. With our third child on the way, I could only hope that somehow I'd find a way to cope.

Motherhood was a great joy but was also peppered with unexpected challenges. Youthful naïvety kept me only a couple of steps ahead of my young children. I was as protective as a lioness of her cubs and would probably have committed murder had anyone laid a hand on any one of them.

As soon as he became mobile, Tony was off, curiosity taking him in all directions, with me close on his heels, retrieving from his mouth a marble or a half-chewed tadpole while anticipating his next potentially treacherous venture.

Our home was seldom silent. We'd indulged in a shiny maple-wood radiogram so I could listen to my treasured record collection: Beethoven, Debussy, Mozart, Bach, opera, ballet, jazz or Broadway – I played them all, so the children heard them all. Within a few years the children's voices were discordantly joining me in singing Christmas carols and adding lusty 'Hallelujahs' to Bach's 'Hallelujah Chorus'.

In a few years, Tony's ear for music soon became evident, his pitch being spot on. It was clear he had inherited the musical talent of his grandfather, who was a pianist, clarinettist and conductor. But it wasn't Beethoven that had him hooked: it was the melodies of Broadway.

In 1964, we moved into our sixth house, and baby number four, our daughter Lynna, arrived.

Jenny, a trained childcarer, moved in to care for the other three children and to feed Candy, our recently acquired corgi, while I was in hospital. Young and capable, she ran the household very competently until I returned. Her playful name for Tony was 'Tony-ony-Macaroni'. It appealed to his sense of fun and became his nickname. As time went by, it evolved. When he was adorable he became Max-a-Million and when he was naughty, Machiavelli.

Two of these nicknames were to re-emerge later in his life. In 1994, Lyle Chan, in his string quartet *An AIDS Activist's Memoir in Music*, dedicated two movements to Tony and named them 'Tony-ony-Macaroni', remembering how Tony had signed his messages of encouragement to Lyle, his fellow activist during the AIDS crisis years. And years later, when he was quite impoverished and saw financial advantage in anonymity, Tony conveniently became the untraceable 'Mr. Max A. Million' on his electricity bills.

Chapter 4

Tone

My spirituality was nurtured by my parents' housekeeper Edna Honeywood (Honey to me) who established in me the importance of God and to care for others with love. Shortly before Honey died, when I was five, she told me I should always do my best to bring pride for my parents and 'This above all, to thine own self be true'. Every day since then I have followed this.

Tony's journal, 1995

1965

Jenny was replaced by the plump, homely and very English Edna Honeywood, who became a part-time family member. I'd don my Carden Constructions secretarial hat and she'd calmly and efficiently take care of the home front. Early every Monday and Thursday morning Tony would wait by the back door, looking forward to a soft-cheeked, grandmotherly cuddle from his new friend, who'd arrive with her ample waist aproned and her fluffy grey hair tied back in a bun. 'Honey' he'd call her, mimicking her Yorkshire accent, which lent an exotic touch of authority to her role. With Jane and Phil at school, Tony relished having Honey to himself, and the pair formed a close, loving and lasting bond. He'd follow her wherever she went, chattering constantly and adamantly refusing to attend pre-school on these days as his brother and sister had done.

One morning Honey walked into the family room and heaved a deep sigh, her blue eyes wide with relief. 'Oooh, thank goodness everything's all right here. Last night I had a terrible dream. Like a nightmare it was, really. The house was a right awful mess, all black and dirty. That light fitting there was dangling down from the ceiling, burnt and broken. Thank goodness it was only a dream. Now come here, Tony, and give me my cuddle.'

Our most recent home had been a source of contention between Keith and me. It had a 'children's wing' at the opposite end of the house from our bedroom. My maternal instinct already had me sleeping with 'one ear open', but this arrangement guaranteed anxious nights. I'd protested but Keith and Bill Baker, our architect, told me the design was all the rage in California, and a sure winner for Sydney's spec house market. So, for the sake of peace, I let it go, knowing my opinion would be disregarded.

A few weeks after moving into the house we celebrated our tenth wedding anniversary. The six of us sat around our candle-lit dinner-table for a celebratory dinner of roast lamb and lemon-delicious-pudding, the children's favourite. Giggling and clinking their glasses of pink lemonade to toasts they proposed to each other, they were already shaping up to be promising party animals.

I tucked them into their beds and, sleepy after several champagnes, began to doze, dreamily aware of a soft crackling sound. Suddenly one-ear-open became brain-on-alert! Dark smoke swirled around us and from the children's end of the house radiated a pulsating orange glow. I shook Keith as my feet hit the floor.

'Quick, the house is on fire!'

'You get the children,' he shouted, running. 'I'll take care of the house.'

Hunched low, heart racing, I stumbled into the smoke-filled family room then through the fire-flickering kitchen, instinct guiding me to the furthest bedroom away: Tony's.

I grabbed his limp body and staggered towards the only easily accessible window, which was in Jane's room. She'd torn a hole in the flyscreen and was wide awake, waiting for me to appear. What a treasure! I leaned out and rolled Tony down onto the grass.

'Climb out and look after him while I get Lynna and Phil', I panted.

I wheezed my way to Lynna's room, grabbed her from her cot, groped my way back and passed her out to Jane. Then I heard Phil's voice from the kitchen: 'Help! Somebody, help me!'

I stood in the doorway, desperately looking into the rolling blackness but little was visible in the smoke-filled kitchen.

'Turn around, Philly,' I called. 'Don't be afraid, just follow Mummy's voice and you'll be safe.' In the calmest voice I could muster I continued calling until, after what must have been minutes but seemed hours, out he stumbled. I threw my arms around him and carried him into Jane's room. Clinging to each other, we climbed out the window, to join the other three children. Somehow we five shaky survivors stumbled our way across the dark lawn, heading towards the porch light of a neighbour's house. I felt no pain when a bone snapped in my foot as Candy the corgi ran between my legs and tripped me up.

'Call the fire brigade!' I panted to Beatrice, our neighbour, who was clearly startled at the sight of a black-faced, nightdress-clad woman with four bedraggled children and a dog in tow. The entire street gradually came to life as dressing-gown-clad neighbours, rubbing their eyes, appeared to investigate the commotion. Firemen arrived, hoses spurted and smoke and steam spilled along the street.

Keith, having correctly guessed that the fire had been electrically ignited, had rushed to turn off the power, only to be flung back onto the grass by an electric shock. He'd staggered to his feet, grabbed a garden hose and was dousing flames through the kitchen window when the 'firies' arrived. Wielding axes, they put out the flames, chopped out the entire kitchen and dragged charred cupboards out onto the grass.

'Those children couldn't have lasted much longer,' the fireman told us. 'You could see where their heads had been lying on their pillows, outlined in black soot. You're all very lucky to be alive.'

The cause of the fire was put down to a transformer near our house producing surges of electricity that had caused a short-circuit in our refrigerator. After lengthy arguments, the electricity provider finally footed the bill for repairs and funded a month's accommodation at a local motel.

In Tony's eyes, Honey's dream showed she possessed special powers, causing his already deep affection for her to soar. In his mind she assumed an oracle-like status.

1967

Dinner was simmering on the stove one afternoon when Keith walked into the kitchen and remarked cheerily: 'I've put the house on the market today because it seems there's a credit squeeze on the way. We'll have to move again to keep up the cashflow. Don't worry, the new spec house is almost finished so we can move into that.'

I'd already decided that next time Keith suggested we move I'd take a firm stand. He was well practised at dropping these loaded bombshells into my lap at a time he hoped would be least likely to provoke a reaction. I turned off the stove and poured a couple of glasses of wine. Dinner could wait.

'We need to talk this over, Keith.'

He flopped into a chair at the kitchen table, his frown revealing his apprehension.

'We can either make this our permanent home or send the children to private schools where they won't need to change schools when we move to a different suburb. Jane's already at her second school and she's finding it quite unsettling.'

I'd done a lot of soul-searching on this issue. Even though I preferred the public system and saw private schools as elitist and overly expensive, I was unwilling to subject our children's education to our itinerant lifestyle. There was a long pause, during which I suspected Keith was making some quick calculations.

'Let's check the figures and see what it would cost. I hear some of the private schools around here are quite good. Why don't you look into it?'

I was amazed to discover long waiting lists for entry into private secondary schools. Apparently, many parents enrol their children at birth, bypassing entry at preparatory level. When my friend Peter Burke, newly arrived from England, investigated the possibility of sending his sons to a private school, he asked the headmaster of a prestigious local boys' school, 'What extra benefits would my sons get for these high fees that they wouldn't get at the local public school?'

'Tone, Mr Burke. They'd get tone,' was the reply.

For Jane, and later Lynna, we chose Chelton Ladies College[3] and for Phil and later Tony, Pennryn College.[4] On the first day of the new term Phil and Jane excitedly donned their new uniforms, Phil flamboyantly sporting his crisp new straw boater, Jane less inspired with her Panama hat and navy gloves. Tony looked on admiringly, impressed by such 'dressing up', and sad to learn that his turn wouldn't arrive for another two years.

We were confident that the schools we'd chosen would provide stability and continuity for our children's education. One lived up to its promise; the other would prove to be a disastrous mistake.

---

3   Pseudonym.
4   Pseudonym.

The innocence you have early in life is so precious and it's easy to have it stripped away . . . which often fuels shame, confusion and a sense of panic that lasts a lifetime.

Richard Glover, *The Sydney Morning Herald Spectrum*,
10 November 2019

Chapter 5

'It'

> When I was a young boy I knew there would be great tragedy in my future. It was destined for me.
>
> Tony's journal, 1995

1969

Tony was up at dawn, dressed and ready long before breakfast, barely able to contain his excitement. The first day of Year 2 at his new 'forever' school, Pennryn College, had at last arrived.

'Hurry up, Philly,' he called out. 'We mustn't be late.'

Tony's beaming face shone from beneath his shiny straw boater, a hat we soon realised we'd be forced to replace at regular intervals when he arrived home with a large bite taken out of its tempting biscuit-like brim.

We were ushered into Pennryn's prep school office to enrol and to meet the headmaster. Tony's uninhibited enthusiasm as he talked about his love of puppet shows brought a smile to the studious, bespectacled Mr Campbell's[5] face.

We wandered past two classroom blocks and eventually, hidden beneath the branches of a shady camphor laurel tree, we spotted a tiny brick cottage. Beside a hibiscus laden with large yellow flowers,

---

5   Pseudonym.

Tony Carden at seven years of age, happy to be going
to his first day of prep school, 1969.

we were amazed to see a continuous line of small boys jumping to the ground from a low window and running along the side of the cottage then back through the door to repeat the circuit, giggling and jostling each other as they went, with no teacher in sight. Then through the trees marched a plump, curly haired lady in a gaudy floral dress, carrying a load of books and a feather duster under her arm.

Miss Gough[6] acknowledged us with a nod and a smile as she took Tony's hand.

'Back to your seats, boys.' Her voice was strong, high-pitched and rang with authority as she brought her young troops to order with a

---
6   Pseudonym.

'It'

few flicks of the feather duster, as it connected randomly with several small bottoms and legs. Tony took to the class of twenty seven-year-olds like a bird to the sky, made two friends, Jeremy and Angus, and adored Miss Gough, who seemed in return to find a soft spot for her new pupil.

From a young age, Tony had an eye for the absurd. Some afternoons he'd rummage with his friends through our dress-ups box at home and emerge as a version of Miss Gough, bedecked in a hand-me-down dress, my feather duster in his hand, mimicking her high-pitched voice. At the end of the year the boys usually took a small gift for their teacher, so I armed him with a box of shortbread and a thank-you card he'd written in his newly acquired running-writing. But that was too mundane for Tony. The next afternoon when we were out shopping, he dragged me into the hardware shop.

'Mummy, have you noticed you've lost your feather duster? You need a new one. I'll help you choose.'

He chose a fluffy pink feather duster to replace the one that had mysteriously gone missing from our kitchen. Years later, I learnt from one of his friends about Tony's unusual Christmas gift to Miss Gough that year. He had painstakingly wrapped the pink feather duster in red cellophane with a card he had made himself sticky-taped to it. Apparently, Miss Gough had been a little taken aback by his facetious gift and when Tony's friends had giggled, she'd given them all a quick leg-flick with her brand-new weapon.

Two years later, the class of twenty had increased to thirty-eight. One of the newcomers was a gentle, softly spoken boy named Andrew Morson, who immediately bonded with Tony. They readily discovered a shared sense of the ridiculous, their zany senses of humour seeing them spending a lot of their leisure time play-acting or making up stories.

Keith was not impressed. 'I'm pretty certain that Morson boy is homosexual,' he said, 'so I don't want him coming here. He's not a good influence on Tony so why don't you do what you can to discourage that friendship?'

I nodded my head but did nothing.

For Keith, Phil was the ideal son. Both heterosexual alpha males, they inevitably developed a strong bond and, to Keith's delight, Phil took enthusiastically to Rugby Union, acquiring two concussions and a broken foot along the way.

But with Tony, it was a different matter. 'Tony, for heaven's sake, pick up the ball and run with it,' Keith would barrack from the sidelines. 'For goodness sake, boy, don't just wander around the field as though you're looking for daisies. Get in there and be part of the action – that's what rugby's all about.'

'I actually think it's better to keep away from the ball, Daddy,' explained Tony, 'because when I get anywhere near it everyone attacks me. What's the point in being attacked? I think rugby's a silly game.'

Tony and his older brother Phil (right),
at a prep school sports carnival, 1970.

'It'

It became increasingly apparent that Keith found it difficult to relate to his second son, the mischievous little boy who enjoyed being cuddled and snuggling into his teddy bear's silky golden fur, and loved bright colours, magic and make-believe.

* * *

In the 1940s and 1950s, during Keith's teenage years, homophobia and chauvinism were clear rites of passage to the brotherhood of masculinity for young men. For some, 'poofter-bashing' was an entertaining sport. Growing up and then working in the building trade, Keith had been well-versed in that environment. Thankfully, his attitudes didn't rub off on Phil: nothing could or ever would change Phil's loyalty to and love for his brother. Phil was Tony's friend and confidante and was always there for him when he needed a shoulder to lean on, regardless of the attitudes of their peers. There was no homophobia there.

Tony was aware that he didn't hit it off with his father in the easy way Phil did, so I tried to make up for this gap in their relationship and reinforce his sense of security within our family circle. Whenever I went into the city I'd visit Coles to buy a miniature china figurine: a little blue-and-white lamb, a cream-and-brown puppy, a pink-and-grey elephant . . . I'd leave it on his dressing table and when he discovered it, he'd say, 'Thank you, Mummy' and give me a hug.

If his siblings noticed these little gifts, they never mentioned them, perhaps because Keith and I took steps to ensure that each of them knew they were loved simply for being themselves – that it was their differences that made them special. When one child needed something, it was provided, but that didn't mean they'd all be given something similar at the same time. They seemed to accept that.

Tony took his china menagerie with him wherever he went through his life as treasured mementos from his childhood.

1971

One morning I blew a kiss to a happy nine-year-old at the school gates and watched him scamper off into the playground, eager as always to catch up with his friends. At three o'clock in the afternoon a changed child waited by the gate, his eyes avoiding mine. The little boy I put my arm around was rag-doll floppy.

Initially I thought it was the onset of one of childhood's dreaded diseases, but no blisters, spots or swelling of the neck emerged. During the night he screamed. I found him sitting bolt upright in bed, shaking, ashen and terrified. When I asked him whether he'd had a nightmare he stared at me blankly. After several more nights of terrors we visited Dr Gunning, our family GP. A thorough examination revealed nothing.

'I think he may be having panic attacks – they're a bit like nightmares, usually related to anxiety,' Dr Gunning offered. 'Perhaps something's happened at school to upset him. Do you know if he has any problems there?'

I shook my head and Tony, when asked, offered no reply. Instead, he hung his head.

I noticed an expression in his eyes I'd not seen before: deep sadness.

'Keep an eye on him and if he's no better next week, bring him back and I'll arrange some blood tests.'

Nothing changed. During the day Tony would brighten up but at night the panic attacks would return. Every morning he was adamant: 'I can't go to school today, Mummy. I'm sick.'

We returned to the doctor for blood tests – everything was normal.

'Something's making him anxious so let's look into it a bit further,' Dr Gunning suggested. 'Perhaps an appointment with a child psychiatrist might help shed some light on whatever's worrying him.'

Phil was worried, too. Every morning he'd encourage Tony to go to school with him, suggesting they could meet for lunch. But Tony

'It'

wouldn't be tempted. He shrugged off any questions with the usual 'I don't know'.

Then one day his answer was different: 'I don't want to talk about it.'

And that's when I first became aware there was an 'it'.

* * *

I didn't doubt that Tony felt loved and appreciated at home because it was to home that he escaped after school, always happy to arrive, so I drew the conclusion that whatever or whoever lay behind his problem, the 'it' he wouldn't discuss was associated with school. It was time I visited Pennryn College.

Mr Campbell showed concern and assured me the staff weren't aware of any problems. The boys in Tony's year were an affable bunch, and Campbell promised me he'd be on the alert for anything amiss.

After three weeks Keith's patience was close to breaking point. He became angry with Tony and reprimanded him: 'You're being a sook and you just need to toughen up, son.'

When this produced no response, out came the razor strop and, despite my protestations, Keith applied his practical solution to Tony's derriere.

'You're going to school tomorrow and that's that.'

The next morning, I delivered Tony directly into the hands of his teacher and for the remainder of the year I accompanied him every morning, hoping for a return of his former zest. His friendships continued to flourish and during out-of-school hours he and his friends seemed as happy together as they'd always been. But he'd changed. Even when he saw a child psychiatrist, Tony doggedly withheld cooperation and the sadness in his eyes lingered on. I was stumped, frustrated that I couldn't help.

I longed for the return of my once-carefree son but as the weeks passed without change, I began to accept that his young life must have taken a destructive turn. But I didn't grasp that the turn was a dark tangent beyond my worst imaginings. Clearly, something had traumatised him and Keith's 'get over it and act like a man' approach hadn't helped. Why wouldn't Tony tell me about it? Did he think I wouldn't understand?

I turned to my own childhood for answers because I, too, had experienced hurt and, like him, I'd kept it to myself. Perhaps that's how many children handle their hurt, especially when it's beyond their comprehension. Perhaps, as did I, Tony would find his own way to escape his problem. During my difficult years I would wander to the back of our garden to talk to my friend the peppercorn tree. I loved that tree. I'd climb into my secret place where the trunk had long ago split in two and sit on its soft grey-brown bark. I shared it with birds and beetles and explored its pungent grey-green leaves, its pendulous bunches of pearly pink peppercorns waiting to be picked and peeled, crunched and sniffed. In the crotch of that gnarled and ancient tree, beneath its feathery foliage, I discovered a substitute for the affection I felt was being withheld: I discovered a deep love for the earth, its mystery and its beauty.

Perhaps Tony needed his own peppercorn tree.

At the Stonewall Inn, a gay bar in New York's Greenwich Village, a riot erupts after patrons attack police who are engaged in routine harassment.

This leads to the birth of the gay liberation and rights movements in the US and elsewhere in the western world.

The Albion Centre, *A HIV/AIDS Timeline*, June 27, 1969

Chapter 6

Escape

My brother's theatrical skills emerged at an early age. His puppet shows had the children of our neighbourhood jockeying for invitations. They'd shriek and squeal at his cheeky, mischievous characters and squirm when sinister villains would appear, created perhaps as an outlet for Tony's own demons. When he changed schools, he blossomed. We had our old Tony back, with a new lease on life. What, I often wondered, had caused the darkness he'd fled from at his previous school?

Jane Mcnab, Tony's sister, 2014

1972

One cold, drizzly winter's morning, I stood on the footpath studying a deserted stately old house on an elegant suburban street. Rain dripped from its grey slate roof. Its red bricks, verandahs on two levels, simply shaped finials, and three chimneys topped with terracotta pots gave it away as Queen Anne style. A tarnished old garden tap had the date 1902 engraved into its pitted brass. A frangipani tree, leafless in winter, spread its branches across the corner of the lower verandah, and I guessed from its size that the tree was of similar vintage to the house. A weathered stone pathway, overgrown with grass and weeds, led to the front steps. The front door featured panels of leadlight glass; beside it was a black plaque engraved with the name 'Greystanes' in brass.

Keith had given me the key:

'I've put a deposit on an acre of land in a fairly upmarket suburb. The land should be good for at least three spec houses, and they should sell like hot cakes because the block's only a stone's throw from the railway station.'

'Sounds great,' I said, impressed with his purchase and wondering where this was leading.

'The problem is there's a rather dilapidated old house on it. Would you mind looking at it when you have a chance? Hopefully you can come up with some ideas about how we could tidy it up. I'll have to flog it off and subdivide the land.'

The large entry hall was dim as I stepped inside but I warmed immediately to the shadowy old house with its high, patterned ceilings, spacious rooms and wide timber staircase. I wandered down the hall into the sprawling kitchen, complete with a walk-in pantry. There was even a buttery.[7] I sensed the long-gone echoes of children's voices. This was a family home, awaiting rebirth. An idea began hatching in my mind. It was time for us to put down roots; the next move would be my twentieth in thirty-six years. Before I'd married I'd lived in nine houses, all rented, and since then, another eleven.

After dinner, I put another proposition to Keith: to make house number twelve our permanent home. He agreed that if Greystanes were to be restored, it would not only become very valuable, but would also provide excellent collateral for the bank.

'You're right, it's time we settled down somewhere,' he concluded. 'We'll do up the old house and live there until the children have left home.'

'Is that a promise, Keith?'

He beamed and gave me a cuddle. I anticipated the years ahead – stable schooling, eighteenth-birthday parties, twenty-firsts, girlfriends and boyfriends coming and going and, best of all, a permanent address.

---

7 A small second pantry for storing drinks.

I Don't Want to Talk About It

From left to right: Keith, Lesley, Tony (having fun wearing a 'mo') and Jane, dining out, 1972.

'Of course, it's a promise.'

Greystanes brought a sense of security I'd not known before. We moved in three days before Christmas, on Tony's eleventh birthday. The following day, he and I were doing some last-minute shopping and as we passed the local pet shop he dragged me back to the window, where a black puppy had taken his eye.

'Look, isn't she beautiful?'

The puppy directed her deep-caramel eyes directly towards me and I glanced at the label. 'Labrador X Beagle – Female – $10.'

'I'd so much like to have a puppy. Please?'

Pleading eyes, a wagging tail and a birthday plea clinched the deal. When Tony arrived home carrying his black bundle, Jane, Phil and Lynna were immediately besotted.

Keith was unimpressed. 'The last thing we need right now is a dog. Who's going to look after it?'

Four hands shot up, and Tony's new acquisition became the most popular present under the Christmas tree. The puppy had the ability to wiggle her backside in the opposite direction to that of her wagging

Tony with birthday puppy Tilly and his cousin, Michael Buck, 1973.

tail, reminding Tony of the tiny waltzing ballerina on top of Lynna's jewellery box.

'She's like a Waltzing Matilda. Let's call her that. She can be 'Tilly' for short.'

Tilly was seldom far from Tony's side. Every night he tenderly took her to the laundry and tucked her into her bed with a ticking clock and a hot water bottle.

'Put a clock in her bed, sonny boy,' the pet shop owner had told him. 'When she hears it ticking, she'll think it's her mother's heart beating and feel safe.'

After numerous arguments between the children, the four upstairs bedrooms were allocated. Phil's claim to the closed-in verandah for his drum kit was readily accepted, while Jane and Lynna settled for the two rooms with walk-in wardrobes. Tony had discovered a tiny attic room, which he found enticingly spooky. He didn't mind having the smallest bedroom; the trade-off was worth it for the low-ceilinged hideaway.

'That little room will make a perfect den,' he beamed, although I had no idea why an eleven-year-old would want a 'den'. Tony did. To him it was a secluded space where a wizard could conjure up magic. It was also a place where he could avenge Lynna for the way Keith favoured her. Keith's disdain of Tony was as palpable as his adoration for his blue-eyed baby daughter, and Tony suffered the pangs of sibling rivalry. Sometimes he'd invite her into his darkened den, where she'd be welcomed by a dancing wizard draped in a colourful cape, a tall, pointy, black-cardboard hat perched on his head. He'd sit her on a chair, blow bubbles from a bubble-pipe, take up his wand and cast spells on his wide-eyed little sister.

'Greystanes' accepted her makeover as graciously as an elegant old lady being dressed for her hundredth birthday, with electrics rewired, ancient plumbing replaced, the old servants' quarters demolished and its Federation-era features refreshed. In February I unearthed the former garden and discovered exotic trees and shrubs, planted years earlier by Professor Eben Gowrie Waterhouse, renowned camellia expert, for his brother, the house's first owner. The latent horticulturist in me revelled in discovering and identifying these old plants, especially when spidery, yellow-throated red flowers appeared and were revealed to be those of the rare, red-flowered climbing lily *Lilium gloriosa*. A rejuvenated garden arose from the bones of its predecessor to the soundtrack of Jane bowing her cello, Lynna tinkling the piano, Tony stroking his violin and Phil's steady drumming, punctuated by an occasional clash of cymbals.

The friendship that continued to develop during these years between Tony and Andrew Morson was strong and would remain lifelong. Andrew's parents, Elizabeth and Stuart, had built a rambling weatherboard house in Castlecrag, nestled beneath a cliff overlooking Middle Harbour, and named it 'Karingal' after Elizabeth's childhood home in Frankston, Victoria. She'd brought seedlings and cuttings from Frankston and planted a garden amongst the gum trees, grevilleas, wattles and waxflowers. By the time Andrew's school friends began visiting Karingal, the sandstone steps to the front door had mellowed to an earthy grey and the twining waxen-flowered hoya vine had woven a network of wiry tendrils over the handrails. During Tony's Pennryn years the house and garden became familiar and dear to him.

The boys would drop their schoolbags, greet Elizabeth with a hug, gobble the teacake or cheese toast she'd prepared and head to the back of the garden for a swim and a couple of hours in boyish dreamland, where they'd invent stories of magic and mayhem. Over several years, their imaginations became more sophisticated, often taking off into the realm of science fiction. Stuart entrusted his movie camera to them and, thanks to his generosity and encouragement, beneath the twisted branches of the angophoras, several of their tales came to life as credible amateur films, one of which won an award. Karingal became Tony's home away from home.

1973

Tony's anxiety continued, along with his listlessness, the restless nights and the panic attacks. He remained steadfast in his refusal to talk about it. Tilly stayed by his side, seemingly sensing his unease and feeling obliged to remain near him. Tony stuck staunchly by Phil, and Phil reciprocated by taking him under his brotherly wing, his own confidence enough for them both. I hoped he might provide a sympathetic ear for Tony to confide in about whatever was amiss at Pennryn. I believed that boys needed to outgrow mother-dependence so I adopted a lower profile and hoped the problem would fade away before the next school year began.

One evening as I was preparing dinner, Tony joined me, glancing around as though to ensure he had me to himself. He pulled up a stool and sat close, with Tilly's head resting against his feet. He seemed more pensive than usual, so I asked him what was on his mind. He looked up, paused a moment as if to contemplate what he was about to say, then pronounced quietly, 'I'm going to kill myself. I've thought about it and I'm going to hang myself off the end of the bed.'

I dropped the spoon and took him in my arms.

'No! Please don't think that way, Tony. You know how much we all love you. You're very important to each one of us and to lots of other people as well. Whatever it is that's making you feel so bad, please just tell me about it because then I can help you to deal with it.'

He let me hold him but said nothing.

The next day I made another appointment with the psychiatrist, hoping that once he understood how serious things had become, he'd find some way to help. Tony adamantly refused to go.

Lynna came to my rescue. 'Mummy, if Tony won't go, I could go instead. There might be things I can tell him about Tony that you don't know.'

Despite last-minute pleas, Lynna and I visited the psychiatrist alone.

'You must realise that unless your son is willing to talk about his problem, it's very difficult for me or, for that matter, anyone to help him,' he told us. 'Tony very clearly has something serious bothering him and he's angry about it. Perhaps he might be more willing to discuss whatever it is that's making him angry with his father or possibly his brother. How does he get along with his dad?'

I hesitated and looked at Lynna. We both knew what Keith thought about 'shrinks'; he knew nothing of our appointment. Coming away with little achieved, I began to consider moving Tony to a different school, for lack of any other solution.

Over the next few weeks, it daunted me to sense in Tony a less enthusiastic response towards situations that had once promised joyful anticipation.

At weekends and after school Tony's imagination, playfulness and creativity provided an escape from whatever it was that hurt and haunted him so. Designing his own puppets occupied his leisure hours. I encouraged and guided him in this not only because it was a fun-filled distraction from his school problem but also compensation for what I saw as a gap in his relationship with Keith. We'd chat as we worked and he'd talk about school and fun times with Andrew, Jeremy and Angus, but never about 'it'.

Our local library became a fruitful source of information, and sometimes Tony would turn to his favourite comic books for ideas for puppet characters, their facial features and their garb. He fashioned heads and necks from plasticine, moulding each face into a character: old, young, hero, heroine, witch or villain. He'd dip pieces of torn tissue paper into paste and work it layer by layer over the plasticine. After it had dried, he'd painstakingly scrape the plasticine out with a spoon, leaving a light but strong, hollow head awaiting transformation into a costumed and painted glove puppet. His favourite part of the process was painting its face into life.

Tony's showmanship skills surfaced very early, along with a determined sense of independence. Soon he had a gallery of puppets, with Phil, Jane and Carolyn providing an audience for his escape into the world of make-believe. Neighbours, teachers, local shopkeepers and even family members were likely targets for Tony's satire. Laughter would explode as he exploited the idiosyncrasies of people whose mannerisms appealed to his sense of humour. Tony's knack for accentuating turns of speech and other quirks that children notice and enjoy mocking made each character recognisable.

It occurred to Keith and me that a puppet theatre could further his hobby. We found one in a local toy shop in the lead-up to Christmas. On Christmas morning four pairs of curious eyes contemplated the bulky package beneath the tree. Eager little hands tore off paper and cardboard to reveal, on top of a stack of pieces of plywood, a glossy picture of a miniature stage.

Tony's eyes widened in disbelief. 'This must be for me! It's for my puppets!'

Phil helped Keith assemble it, but the pale plywood looked like an under-baked scone, so Jane fetched her acrylic paints and she and Tony brought it to life. Across the top of its arching facade large vermillion letters announced 'TONY-ONY-MACARONI PUPPET SHOW'.

Word soon passed along the prep school students' and mothers' grapevines that Tony Carden's puppet theatre was available for birthday parties. Talk of wizards and monsters had little boys begging their mothers to add Tony's puppet show to their birthday party plans. Mothers would willingly do so, relieved to have a diversion for their birthday-party-sugar-fuelled sons.

As Tony would learn in later years, an actor has three main tools for communicating with an audience: hands, eyes and voice. He was abundantly skilled in using all three. He learnt to manipulate his long fingers inside his glove puppets, gently or with vigour, as the occasion

Year 4 class photo, prep school, 1972. Tony, second from the left in the front row, is troubled with a secret he doesn't want to talk about.

required, and although his eyes were not visible to his audience his voice, already showing promise as a fine actor's tool, commanded attention with its extensive range and appealing timbre. Cheering, hooting and booing prevailed, and best of all everyone including the puppeteer had fun. Tony happily accepted increasingly frequent invitations to perform for his audiences of eager eight- and nine-year-olds. His only request was that the party-hostess provide transport, something that ensured the independence that even at eleven meant so much to him.

We settled into six relaxing summer-holiday weeks of taking Tilly for walks, visiting the beach and spending time with friends. As another school year loomed, Tony became quiet and pensive. His anxiety returned along with a picky appetite.

'I don't want to go back to Pennryn this year,' he announced at dinner one night. 'Could I please go to a different school?'

Quickly I jumped in: 'You could go to the local high school. It's co-ed and you might like that better.'

I anticipated from his expression and intake of breath that Keith was about to deliver the 'no' word, so I hastily continued. 'I think changing schools would be a good idea for you, Tony. You haven't been happy at Pennryn for a long time now so let's look into it, shall we?'

Keith looked disappointed but my gut feeling told me that whatever Tony's problem was, he'd found his own solution – without needing to reveal 'it'. The happy son I'd lost two years ago returned soon after the decision was made.

Things were finally looking up.

When a man's heart wakes and his body too, they can be bent this way or that, as the wind bends a sapling. But after a while the sapling stiffens and grows hard as a tree. Then it cannot be bent any more, but grows to its own shape.

            Morris West, *The Devil's Advocate*

Chapter 7

Betrayed

> Tony, we all knew, was going to be a star. The theatre of life would become his ultimate medium.
>
> Simon Hunt, school friend, 1995

1974

The new school year saw Tony exchange train travel with Phil for short bus trips with local youngsters and previously mandatory rugby for tennis and basketball.

After school and at weekends, new schoolfriends appeared, both girls and boys, and within a few months Jane, Phil and Lynna were joining the fun. When Andrew and other Pennryn friends visited, they too became part of the more spontaneous leisure regime.

The Tony-ony-Macaroni Puppet Theatre gained a new audience and its performances lightened into more slapstick routines.

Best of all, from my perspective, was to see the shadow of 'it' gradually receding.

They were happy days, but they were not to last . . .

* * *

One wintery afternoon Keith dropped home for a warm-up coffee.

'Sign this please,' he said offhandedly, handing me a document and a pen.

'What is it?'

'Oh, nothing important, just another routine document from the bank.'

My hand shook as I read with disbelief a contract for the sale of our home.

'How could you do this?' I demanded.

Keith said nothing.

'What about Tony? If we move from here, he'd have to leave his new school. He's so happy there now after those difficult years at Pennryn. You can't do that to him, Keith. It wouldn't be fair.'

'He'll go back to Pennryn,' Keith replied.

I glared at him through my tears, making no attempt to hide the fury and resentment I was feeling. He looked terrified but stood his ground. I wanted to tear up the contract and throw it back at him, but instead, feeling as though I'd been punched, I signed it. I'd been deceived and defeated, but the deal had already been done. I should have taken a tougher stand.

Six weeks later we moved into house number thirteen, the first on a new estate in a growing suburb. The agent with whom Keith had colluded tried to make light of it by telling me how lucky I was to have a succession of new houses to enjoy.

'Yes,' I bitterly responded, 'but they're houses, not homes. There's a difference, you know.'

Despite his and my pleas, Tony returned to Pennryn, but his heart was elsewhere. He'd been spared the teenage anguish of acne as his shoulders broadened. His hair remained golden and set off his perfectly arched dark brows and even, white teeth, looks that stood him in good stead as an aspiring actor but were a target for the bullies at school. He had a natural grace and rhythm, something that aroused homophobia in some of the more macho boys, but as ever, Phil was there.

'Get lost, mate! Mess with my brother and you mess with me!' Phil made an example of one particular bully, pinning him against the wall and swinging a couple of punches close by his face. When Phil was called to the headmaster's office to be interrogated about the confrontation, he told Dr Hastings the boy had deserved it.

'He had it coming, sir. He was a bully, and someone had to do something about it.'

'If you were still in prep school, Carden, you'd get one hundred acquisitions,' the headmaster proclaimed, 'but you're not and you should know better by now, so watch your behaviour, son.'

'One hundred acquisitions' was Pennryn prep school's standard punishment for most misdemeanours, requiring the guilty party to write out one hundred times: 'The acquisition of self-discipline is an integral part of the curriculum of Pennryn Preparatory School.' The lines were due on the headmaster's desk on the following Monday morning and usually took the penitent an entire weekend to complete. There were few repeat offenders.

* * *

Plum parts in Pennryn's annual school plays and musicals were much sought after, bestowing the kudos of performing in productions highly regarded among Sydney's private schools' well-reputed drama circles. Tony spent much of his spare time, after meeting his academic requirements, studying scripts and learning lines in preparation for auditions. He worked hard and it paid off: he was rewarded with roles in Dylan Thomas's *Under Milk Wood* and Broadway's *Oklahoma*. The opportunities Pennryn offered in drama combined with the excellence of its English literature program stood Tony in good stead throughout his life.

Every Saturday Tony checked the TV guide to see which old black-and-white movies and musicals were programmed. He discovered Bette Davis and Marilyn Monroe, James Dean and Marlon Brando,

Fiddler on the Roof, West Side Story, Hair and *Jesus Christ Superstar.* He'd chat with me about them, knowing I shared his passion for song and dance. I told him of how, when *Hair* had premiered in Sydney in 1969 with its full-frontal male nudity, it was considered the wildest theatre ever to hit the Sydney stage. And how, when I'd bought tickets as a surprise for Keith's birthday, certain we'd both enjoy it, he'd 'rescued us from depravity' by exchanging the tickets for Gilbert and Sullivan's *HMS Pinafore.* He'd persisted in viewing me as 'twinset and pearls', but the world was changing and so was I.

Tony's TV-viewing habits irritated Keith, who believed boys' leisure time was better spent outdoors kicking balls or riding bikes. He accused Tony of becoming a lounge lizard.

'One day I'm going to New York to study acting. I'm planning to become an actor on Broadway,' Tony responded. 'So, I'm not wasting time, I'm actually studying for my career.'

Touché.

1975

At the age of fifteen Tony took a first decisive step towards fulfilling his ambition. He enrolled at a weekend drama program at the Independent Theatre in North Sydney with his friends Itty and Hugo. Tony made his debut in a Saturday matinee performance of *You're a Good Man, Charlie Brown* in the lead role, with Hugo as Assistant Director.

Although we remained together for several years afterwards, my marriage to Keith didn't survive the sale of Greystanes and Tony's return to Pennryn. I couldn't forgive his deceit and, once alerted to it, discovered it went further than the sale of our home. Feeling that I could never trust him again, I applied for a divorce in mid-1976. I sensed the trauma I was causing our children when I saw the pain and panic in Tony's eyes. They were all devastated, but at fourteen, and because he carried 'it' in his heart, Tony was probably the most vulnerable.

A simple, white, aluminium-clad timber cottage with two bedrooms and a small study became our new home, a tight squeeze for Jane, Lynna, Tony and me and necessitating the creation of a mini-bedroom at the back of the garage. Phil chose to remain with Keith and for overnight stays we set up a folding bed.

It was all I could afford with my meagre $30,000 divorce settlement. A local plant nursery employed me, thanks to the certificate in horticulture I'd recently acquired, and we lived a simple life, not geographically far from 'Greystanes' but a world away from its luxury. In order to be at home during after-school hours I upgraded my nursery job to become a plant quarantine officer on Sydney's waterfront, which was quite a contrast from the building industry, although both had similar 'weird mob' cultures, as parodied by Nino Culotta in his book about the Australian building industry's migrant workforce, *They're a Weird Mob*. Working on Sydney's waterfront necessitated turning a blind eye to wharfies' girlie calendars and a deaf ear to much of the language, but I found most of the men to be 'salt of the earth' types, full of unexpected kindnesses.

* * *

In mid-1977 auditions were held at Pennryn for roles in the end-of-year's upcoming musical *Bye Bye Birdie*. The headmaster was to be producer and he appointed Mark Young,[8] an experienced and highly qualified drama teacher, as director. The school orchestra was flourishing under the musical leadership of Robert Cross[9] and everything was shaping up well for a promising production. Our tiny home began to ring to the strains of 'Put on a Happy Face', 'A Lot of Livin' to Do' and 'Rosie' as Tony prepared for his audition. The afternoon of the

---

8   Pseudonym.
9   Pseudonym.

audition, he came home from school and walked in the door with a beaming smile.

'How'd it go?'

'Did you get a part?'

'Tell us.'

'You'll never believe it. They said I was really good. I've got the lead role.'

His happiness was heartening. When Jane and Lynna teased him, he retorted, 'Shut up. One day I'll be famous and you'll have to pay to drink my bathwater.'

'Don't use too much soap,' they chortled. 'We can hardly wait.'

One September afternoon Tony arrived home from school later than usual.

'Where've you been? Isn't this rather late to be getting home?' I quizzed him.

'I've been rehearsing for *Bye Bye Birdie*.'

That surprised me. Then the following week, when he arrived home even later, I wondered why the school's orderly scheduling of rehearsals had changed. This continued for two more weeks, and when one afternoon Tony arrived home at six o'clock with traces of make-up on his face, I exploded.

'Tony, what on earth is going on? I know Pennryn doesn't keep you this late so where have you been? And what's the make-up about?'

'I've been at Mr Young's place. He's been giving me extra dance lessons and teaching me how to use stage make-up because he wants to help me do my part well.'

I had a mental picture of what private dance lessons and make-up applications might entail and felt uncomfortable about it, so I consulted Keith.

'You're being over-protective. Tony is fifteen now. Besides, he's got a big part so maybe he does need some extra help.'

Unconvinced, I called Pennryn to schedule an appointment, took a day off work, and went to see the headmaster.

'Dr Hastings, Tony has told me that Mr Young's been taking him home after school for extra lessons. I'm not happy about that. Shouldn't all this be happening here at school?'

'I think you're just being an over-anxious mother, Mrs Carden,' Dr Hastings replied. 'Mr Young's a very conscientious director as well as an excellent drama and dance teacher. The students think the world of him. He's putting a great deal of effort into our musical. I'm sure there's nothing to worry about.'

I felt I'd been told the equivalent of 'Go home, bake a chocolate cake and calm down.'

Three weeks later Keith was summoned to Dr Hastings's office on a different matter: Phil had been caught smoking. Marijuana? Keith was livid. He confronted Phil for an explanation, scathingly remarking, 'This is all I need. One son's a poofter and now the other's a druggie.'

Phil countered the accusation by offering an inventive explanation and Keith, after discussing this issue with the headmaster, took the opportunity to air his displeasure at Mark Young's 'after-school lessons'. Keith was satisfied that their chat had cleared the air. However, nothing had changed.

Not quite defeated, I decided to ask Tony to invite Mark home for afternoon tea. I greeted him at the front door and left them chatting in the lounge room while I went to make tea. He was slim, probably in his late twenties, relaxed and casually charming. I could see why the cast enjoyed working with him. He had charisma. Aiming for a diplomatic approach, I took the plunge: 'Tony's told me about the extra lessons you're giving him for *Bye Bye Birdie*. It's very generous of you, Mr Young, but I'd feel more comfortable if you'd do it here rather than taking Tony to your place.' I exhaled a huge sigh of relief and with it released the tension that had almost choked me.

'It's like this, Mrs Carden. There's plenty of space to work at my place. And we need space to rehearse. Looking around here, I doubt there's enough room.'

With Tony nodding in agreement, my anger increased as I realised that not only was I powerless, but that Tony was complicit.

'We need a big area to rehearse, Mum,' he added. 'Just imagine the size of a stage and you'll understand. There's no way we could do it here.'

I accepted that my concern was a lost cause but remained unconvinced.

Over the next few weeks, Tony often asked me to pick him up late in the afternoon from a dilapidated old mansion on the main road where he'd wait for me on the footpath, telling me that he went there 'to listen to music with friends'. I couldn't help but wonder whether one of his 'friends' was Mark and whether the old building housed Mark's 'studio'. At fifteen Tony had assumed control of his own life.

Bye Bye Birdie was a huge success. The production achieved commendation from the Australian Council of the Arts, and Tony received an award from the Arts Council of New South Wales. I was excited for him, and proud, but my mother's intuition still gnawed at me. Something was not right.

New Homosexual Disorder Worries Officials

A serious disorder of the immune system that has been known to doctors for less than a year ... a disorder that appears to affect primarily male homosexuals ... has now afflicted at least 335 people.

The New York Times, 11 May 1982

Chapter 8

The Blue Suitcase

> I say throw caution to the wind and strive for everything. Who knows what tomorrow will bring? One must always strive for happiness today.
>
> Tony's journal, 1995

1978

A few weeks after *Bye Bye Birdie* wrapped up, Tony devised a way to escape Pennryn again, this time for good. 'I'd like to apply to become an AFS exchange student next year. Scott Whitmont just got back. He stayed in America with a really great host family, and he thinks I'd have a pretty good chance of being selected.'

The Whitmonts lived nearby and although I knew Scott often travelled with Tony to school, I hadn't realised he'd been away, so I asked Tony about AFS.

'AFS stands for American Field Service and it started during World War I,' he explained. 'Apparently a group of young Americans who were living in Europe during the war decided they'd like to help out in some way so they volunteered to drive ambulances. Later, AFS evolved into an international exchange student program.'

'Are you sure you'd want to spend a whole year away with another family? That mightn't be easy.'

'I'm absolutely certain,' Tony replied. 'If I can find an after-school job and save half the money, would you be willing to pay the other half? I really want to go to America.'

Those brimming-with-enthusiasm eyes couldn't be refused. We filled out application forms and coaxed statements from family members, school friends and teachers. Working as a waiter at Pancakes on the Rocks soon saw Tony's savings mount and after months of interviews and aptitude tests, he was accepted as an AFS exchange student for the 1979/1980 program, with the US his first preference.

Meanwhile, Pennryn lived up to its reputation as a leading school in dramatic arts. Tony, with his characteristic zeal, landed himself more roles. He played Don Quixote in *Man of La Mancha* and as he sang 'The Impossible Dream', there were tears in my eyes, because that's what I thought he might have.

Later in the year I remarried. Jim Saddington and I had become friends several years earlier when we'd studied horticulture together. Younger than me, Jim was a tall, sturdy plantsman, a green-fingered horticulturist, with a mop of frizzy auburn hair; his brown eyes expressing sincerity and a guilelessness that saw only life's goodness. At our wedding Jane sang a love song that she and Lynna had written, while Lynna accompanied her on guitar, as we cut the blue-iced cake decorated with daisies lovingly made by my childhood friend Maureen. It took time, in fact several months, for Jane, Phil, Tony and Lynna to accept Jim, but eventually he gained their trust with his sincerity and became their big-brotherly friend.

As the months of waiting rolled by, Tony and his friend Andrew grabbed every opportunity to put Stuart's movie camera to good use, honing their movie-making skills in Elizabeth's garden. Both boys were keenly aware that they would miss each other when Tony left for the US. Their bond was strong and secure and had been their anchor during their Pennryn years.

Tony's love for Stuart and Elizabeth was mutual. Stuart had taken Tony under his fatherly wing, probably sensing, after attending

Tony with friend Itty (Felicity Copeland) at his farewell party before heading to the USA as an exchange student, Sydney, 1979.

Pennryn's junior rugby matches, that Tony's relationship with Keith was frail.

'Tony, Dad has something for you, and he's asked me to invite you over on Saturday after sport. Can you come?' Andrew looked excited.

So on Saturday afternoon, Tony went to the Morsons and knocked on the door of Stuart's office, the one room in the house he'd not entered before.

'Come on in, Tony. I'm glad you could come. How was rugby today?'

'We're only Grade Three, but we played against St Leo's and it was a draw, so it didn't go too badly,' replied Tony, taking in the office: books, lots of books, wide open windows with expansive views, a polished reddish-brown timber desk and an impressive row of black-framed medical degrees on the wall.

'Congratulations on being selected as an exchange student, Tony,' said Stuart, shaking Tony's hand. 'I'm sure you'll be a great ambassador for Australia when you're over in the US. Remember that I'm always here if you ever need an extra ear to bounce things off. Here, I have something for you.'

Stuart reached beneath his desk and produced a large parcel wrapped in brown paper and tied with a red ribbon. He placed it on the desk in front of Tony.

'Oh, thank you, Dr Morson. I don't really know what to say,' said a surprised Tony as he carefully untied the ribbon and tore away the paper to reveal a dark-blue leather suitcase with the initials 'TC' inscribed in gold on its lid.

'It's beautiful! And it's Pennryn blue! Thank you so very much. We've been wondering whether we had the right bag for a whole year in America, but this is just amazing. It's perfect!' He hugged Stuart, who had a tear in his eye.

'Bon voyage, Tony. Please try to find time to write.'

Andrew admired Tony's new blue suitcase with heaviness in his heart, sensing the spontaneity of their friendship was about to change.

Tony's departure would bring to a close the years they'd shared in Karingal's bushland hideaway, the oasis where they'd cemented the bond that had sustained them throughout the challenges of their school days.

T.S. Eliot's *Murder in the Cathedral* was Pennryn's major dramatic production for 1979 and was to be staged a few weeks before Tony's departure. Determined not to miss this last opportunity, Tony spent hours studying the script and rehearsing excerpts in readiness for the auditions. Once again, success! He landed the principal role: Thomas à Becket.

The vaulted ceiling of the school chapel provided the perfect setting for the production, its Gothic-style stained-glass windows casting golden light over the pulpit and altar, a made-to-order stage. The audience sat congregation-style in wooden pews.

A blue brocade robe over his white cassock, an archbishop's mitre poised regally on his head, Tony, as Thomas, imparted to his congregation that soon they may have another martyr, a foreboding message, not only for Thomas, but also for Tony.

Tony as the Scarecrow in *The Wizard of Oz*,
with his host parents Elaine and Bill Stennard, St Louis, 1980.

His performance earned him an award from the National Institute of Dramatic Art (NIDA), a much sought-after prize endowing the recipient with a foot-in-the-door future in Australian theatre. Tony left Pennryn with two 'Blues' for drama emblazoning the pockets of his school blazer and a heart full of hope for what the year overseas might hold in store.

* * *

The pale glow of a clear winter sunrise brightened into morning as we headed to Kingsford Smith Airport. Tony was headed to St Louis, Missouri, where he would be met by the Stennard family: Elaine, Tom, and their three children Karen, Tom Junior, who was Tony's age, and Richard, the youngest. He'd been matched with the Stennards, from Chesterfield, Missouri, because nearby Parkway Central High, his school for the coming year, strongly featured music and drama in its curriculum. The year away would culminate in Tony's graduation ceremony.

It was time. We all gave Tony a quick hug before he joined other animated, eager seventeen-year-olds filing into the customs hall. Tony turned back to call, 'Please look after Tilly for me.'

As the weeks progressed, regular letters from Tony and Elaine assured me that Tony and the Stennard family were well matched.

Towards the middle of the year when their daughter Karen was diagnosed with a form of blood cancer, I offered to request that AFS consider a replacement family for Tony. Both Elaine and Karen vehemently declined, insisting that Tony's cheery presence not only eased their anxiety but that his bond with Karen had become her mainstay during her chemotherapy. By the end of Tony's exchange year Karen's illness was in remission and her friendship with Tony ongoing.

During their time overseas, every AFS exchange student was given the opportunity to experience a different community during the end-of-year break from the one where they had spent the rest of

Tony at his graduation ceremony from
Parkway Central High, St Louis, June 1980.

the year. Tony worked his charms on the AFS staff, manipulating and manoeuvring to get himself to New York City. Being Tony, he succeeded. His Long Island hosts spent a rollercoaster three weeks showing him around, spurred on by his extreme enthusiasm, and taking well-earned respite on days when Tony took the bus to explore alone. It wasn't long, but it was time enough for him to set in motion some plans for his future: he found the Lee Strasberg Theatre and Film Institute, where he picked up a prospectus. He then located a solicitor, Leonard Krait,[10] suggested by a contact at Pennryn, to discuss his other near-impossible dream: United States residency. He'd made no mention of this to us. We all assumed he'd be happy to start his career as most aspiring Australian actors did: either at Sydney's NIDA or the Western Australian Academy of Performing Arts (WAAPA).

But Tony's horizons were broader.

---

10 Pseudonym.

1980

Back at the airport a year later, anxious but excited families inspected the procession of returnees trundling their luggage down the exit ramp from the customs hall. Everyone crowded together, trying to recognise sons, daughters, brothers and sisters after a year away. Some of the returned travellers, having enjoyed the US diet, had changed shape; others sported new hairstyles; a few had acquired a distinctly American dress sense, but eventually each ship found its mooring and there were hugs and kisses galore as we welcomed them home. The year away had matured Tony. He looked more a man than a boy and sported a broad American accent.

Back home, Tilly was waiting by the front gate, her tail wagging in a frenzy as she leapt into Tony's open arms, the past year having just shrunken in her mind into a dog's long day. Tony had changed in subtle ways I couldn't attribute to maturity or to spending a year in a different culture: the way he moved his body when he walked, his choice of tight jeans, his distancing from us – these were all new.

Tilly, 1978.

A few days after his return, as Jane, Phil, Lynna, Jim and I were sitting around the fire toasting marshmallows, Tony emerged from his room wearing a black plastic jumpsuit, a Mickey Mouse hat and clear-plastic platform shoes. We were agog. Where was the fancy-dress party?

'I'm off to the city to find some fun,' he said casually. 'I'd forgotten how boring it is here.'

As the door closed after him, guffaws of laughter filled the room. Wherever would he go, dressed like that, to 'find some fun'?

A week later Tony announced that rather than audition for NIDA he intended to look for a job.

'I don't intend to go to NIDA[11] and I don't want to go to WAAPA[12], either, so don't hassle me. The US is the best place in the world to study acting and that's where I intend to go.'

From left to right: Lesley, Jim Saddington, Tony, Lynna, Jane and Phil, relaxing at home, Sydney, 1980.

---

11 NIDA (National Institute of Dramatic Art)
12 WAAPA (Western Australian Academy of Performing Arts)

'But why not take advantage of the award you've already won from NIDA?' I argued. 'You could study there at a fraction of the cost, and you wouldn't be forking out for somewhere to stay – you can stay here rent-free. Just think how hard it would be over there, and lonely, too, without us to lend a helping hand when you need one.'

But his mind was made up. The following week he showed up at David Jones ready to start work as a shop assistant in the menswear department, and, on Friday nights and weekends, he donned a black apron for his transformation into a waiter at a city restaurant.

Knuckling down to this demanding routine, Tony had soon saved enough to bid Sydney's outer suburbia a not-so-fond farewell. He moved to Darlinghurst, an inner-city suburb with a vibrant nightlife, to flat-share with Andrew.

* * *

For my generation, awareness of homosexuality was scant, almost non-existent. I'd heard the tragic story of Oscar Wilde and lamented that a judgemental society could so rudely intrude into people's privacy, but otherwise I'd given it little thought. My awareness was largely limited to the scathing way some Australian men, including Keith, referred to 'poofters', a prejudice I instinctively resented. I remembered Terry, a friend from my teenage years, who'd suddenly announced he was leaving Australia to live in England. I'd assumed at the time that he was seeking greener pastures to pursue his editing and publishing career. Years later Terry told me that the real reason for his departure wasn't his career but that he was gay, something his clergyman father would never have handled. For love of his father he'd kept his sexuality private.

'Homosexual' seemed such a cold, clinical-sounding term. When 'gay' replaced it, I felt its image had been lightened to encompass the meanings joyful and carefree, bright and showy. I thought the gay community had done rather well in adopting this new term.

* * *

After our divorce, Keith had moved to country Bethungra, near Cootamundra, where he and Connie, his new wife, had bought the historic Shirley Hotel. When he visited Sydney, he and I would meet up with Tony for lunch and a catch-up chat. At one of our lunches, on a whim, I asked Tony about his sexuality, vaguely thinking it might be something he'd want to reveal to Keith and me when we were together. I should have realised that to broach the subject in Keith's presence was foolhardy. His answer to my clumsily worded question was the stock response of the time: 'No, I'm not. And why do you want to know, anyway?'

I wished desperately that I knew why I wanted to know. If he'd answered 'yes', I know I would have been sad. It would have meant that he was part of a minority group, frowned on by society, subject to discrimination and that he'd miss out on the joys of fatherhood. But Tony was my son and I would have accepted it – and him – with love.

My blunder widened the gap between us. What had begun as a crack when his Pennryn trauma had driven him to secrecy now broadened to a chasm: vast, deep and clogged with misunderstanding. Perhaps he'd have preferred it to stay that way, to keep that distance between us, and that's where it may have ended. But years later, his spirit beckoned me, and I followed, embarking on a confronting journey down to the bottom of the chasm and back up, to reach him again, just in time.

1981

Compared to sleepy suburbia, Tony and Andrew's flat on the top floor of a high-ceilinged old house in Darlinghurst was decidedly cosmopolitan. The two young men busied themselves creating an 'arty' décor for their 'pad': ruby-red crushed velvet curtains added mystique to the archway into the living area, and bowls of feathers and potpourri graced the windowsills.

One Monday, when their days off coincided, they invited Elizabeth and me to a lunch of garlic-and-prawn pasta followed by elegant parfaits in tall glasses. Impressed by our sons' culinary skills, we grinned with satisfaction that we'd trained them so well. However, much of the credit belonged to Andrew, who'd joined Sydney Opera House's catering team.

Another frequent visitor to the house was Andrew's dark-haired boyfriend George, a Qantas steward. Tony got along well with George and was pleased to see Andrew and George enjoying their new relationship. He left them to their socialising because nothing could distract him from his goal to save for his return to New York.

'Well, I've done it,' he announced one day on a visit to my house in March 1982. 'I've got a good deal on a cheap flight and I'm off in three weeks. I don't want anyone to worry about me, especially you, Lezzles,' he said, chuffed that he'd remembered my father's nickname for me.

'Of course I'll worry,' I insisted. 'You'll need accommodation as soon as you arrive and finding it might not be easy.'

'Friends of the Stennards, Jenny and Austin Myers, live in suburban New York and they've agreed to let me stay with them until I can get on my feet, so I'll be okay. I'll give you the address, so please make sure everyone writes. That'll be really important to me because even though this is something I want to do, I'm going to miss you all terribly.'

'Of course we'll all write,' I replied. 'And we'll look after Tilly, too.'

'Yes, I've been trying to work out a way to take her with me, but it's just not possible. It's far too expensive. Anyway, I suppose she really belongs to all of us now.'

Three weeks later he was packed and ready to go. He popped back home for a send-off. To the strains of Franks Sinatra's 'New York, New York' we clinked glasses and joined in the chorus 'If you can make it there you'll make it anywhere, it's up to you, New York, New York', as Tony plunged a knife into the stars-and-stripes-iced, sparkler-topped farewell cake that Andrew had baked and decorated. Andrew's sadness was matched by Elizabeth's.

In tears and after a farewell hug for his beloved old dog, Tony was off again, this time for the long haul.

Watching the plane shrink to a dot in the sky and then disappear altogether, we had no idea how tragic his timing would prove to be. Blithely anticipating being out of the 'closet' and away from scrutiny, Tony was heading towards a calamity of catastrophic proportions brewing for America's gay community.

1982

No-one would be there to greet the twenty-year-old Tony Carden when he landed in New York City, exhilarated about his adventure and eager to put the wheels of his new life into motion. He would be reliant on the kindness of his two pre-arranged contacts and a generous dose of support from Lady Luck. From here on, communication with us would be only by short reverse-charge phone calls and whatever letters he'd find time to write.

To pursue an acting career in the US was what Tony saw as his destiny. The seed of his ambition had germinated years earlier, nurtured by the music and movies of Broadway; it had sprouted into fruitful promise when he heard about the Lee Strasberg Theatre and Film Institute. That would be the school for him, where he'd be following in the footsteps of many of the world's greatest actors. Enthused by his thespian successes at Pennryn, he'd heeded the advice from mentors there, which he valued far more than that of his well-meaning but not so theatre-savvy family, who could offer only obstacles to his American dreams.

1,112 and Counting!

If this article doesn't scare the shit out of you, we're in real trouble.

If this article doesn't rouse you to anger, fury, rage and action, gay men may have no future on this earth. Unless we fight for our lives, we shall die.

When we first became worried, there were only 41 cases of AIDS. In only twenty-eight days there were 164 new cases – and 73 more dead. For the first time, doctors are saying out loud and up front 'I don't know'. Hospitals are now so filled with AIDS patients that there is often a waiting period of up to a month before admission and suicides are now being reported.

If all this had been happening to any other community for over two long years, there would have been, long ago, such an outcry from that community and all its members that the government of this city and this country would not know what had hit them.

Let's talk about hospitals. Everybody's full up, fellows. No room at the inn.

There are increasing numbers of men unable to work and unable to claim welfare because AIDS is not on the list of qualifying disability illnesses. People are being thrown out onto the street with nowhere to live and no money to live with.

Get your stupid heads out of the sand, you turkeys. I don't want to die and I can only assume you don't want to die. Can we fight together?

Larry Kramer, US playwright and founder of
Gay Men's Health Crisis, *New York Native*, 1983

Chapter 9

Children and Art

I know all I must do in the next few years but I want to do it all tomorrow. It is a long journey I have ahead of me but with a lot of hard work and some help from my friends, I know I can accomplish my goals, maybe even more.

Tony's postcard, June 1982

1982

A few weeks after Tony's departure, a bulky, New York City–postmarked, brown-paper envelope arrived in our letter box. Prior to that, all we'd had from Tony was a short phone call letting us know he'd arrived safely.

> Dear Lezzles,
> Life has been flat to the floor every hour since I arrived ... The Lee Strasberg Institute has produced many of the acting greats of our time – Marilyn Monroe, James Dean, Marlon Brando ... [There are] no levels of tuition, no beginning or end, you join classes with actors who have achieved, are achieving and hopefully will achieve. Following the beliefs of the great Stanislavski, it's called Method Acting ... I'll need all the help I can get both financially and emotionally. I have a gut feeling this is what I must do and this is where I must do it.

Jenny and Austin have been very welcoming and they've kindly offered to let me stay a few more months – meanwhile I'm looking for share accommodation in Manhattan . . . I don't think Keith sees how difficult all this is. Finding it hard to make ends meet, working in a bar, doing a lot of socialising and meeting people who are very beneficial contacts. I've been invited to a big party at Studio 84 to celebrate *A Chorus Line*'s long run as a New York musical. New York people really know how to enjoy themselves – guests like Andy Warhol, Cary Grant, Gina Lollobrigida . . .

Love to everyone . . . Tony-oni-Macaroni

He'd wasted no time during those first few weeks – we wondered how he found time to sleep, let alone search for new accommodation.

Every apartment he could afford fell far short of meeting what he considered basic living standards. They were small-windowed, dime-in-the-slot-heated bed-sitters, five to eight flights of stairs up, with the

Manhattan Card Shop where Tony worked 1982/5.

Tony Carden in his casting agency photo, New York, 1982.

odour of stews and curries drifting up the spiral stairway to stifle the appetites of those at the top.

He and Leonard Krait, the solicitor he'd consulted about seeking residency, had become friends.

'You're welcome to move in here,' Leonard offered. 'There's a spare bed in the loft. You're good company so I'd enjoy having you around.'

Done deal!

Life became settled after he moved to Leonard's gracious brownstone apartment. He was now living in the 'arty' part of town, not far from Broadway and the Lincoln Center for the Performing Arts and, best of all, within walking distance of the Lee Strasberg Institute. Understanding Tony's need to save for tuition fees, Leonard charged him no rent.

Opening-night parties, promotional events and music gigs were part of the life of Broadway. As a silver-service waiter and an experienced barman, Tony was soon snapped up to work at parties and press performances for actors, musicians, theatre companies and entrepreneurs. He worked by night, attended acting classes and singing lessons by day and, in whatever time he had left over, worked for Maree Carlos,[13] an Australian jeweller. With no rent to pay and the gigs paying well, the extra work soon saw his savings mount, so he decided to take a short trip back home with Leonard during Strasberg's mid-semester break.

* * *

It was the evening of my birthday. The chatter of diners mingled with the clinking of glasses as waiters glided between tables in an inner-city Greek restaurant. Suddenly something brushed against my neck. As I raised my hand to slap what I thought to be an insect, a necklace was gently lowered over my head.

'Happy Birthday, Lezzles.'

I thrilled at the sound of the dear, familiar voice, and as Tony's infectious laughter spread across the room, other diners who'd seen him creep up behind me joined the frivolity.

'Tony! I can't believe it's you. What a fantastic surprise.'

He had made the necklace himself, using his newly acquired jewellery-making skills. How I treasure it still, with its seashells and fresh-water pearls.

* * *

When AIDS first caught the attention of Sydneysiders, it was only a background whisper. People joked about it, as though being flippant

---

13 Pseudonym.

might keep it at bay. At a Christmas party, when I was asked for advice about the host's wilting pot plant, a guest remarked: 'Maybe it's got AIDS.' This was followed by guffaws of laughter.

In the early hours I'd lie awake, wondering, worrying: Tony was over there in the midst of it all. How aware was he? How careful? Although he'd never come out, we'd accepted he was gay, so I tried to keep abreast by learning what little I could from the newspapers.

In March 1983 Australia had a new government. Dr Neal Blewett, politically open-minded, seemed a promising choice as the new Minister for Health. If AIDS reached our shores, surely the Australian government's response would be better than that of the US government? Anxiety there was on the rise. By 1981, the US Department of Health and Human Services' weekly 'Morbidity and Mortality' score had revealed that the infection rate had risen rapidly. And the US Government was turning a blind eye.

* * *

Towards the end of 1983, I sensed from Tony's letters that something had changed. Disinclined to ask Tony, I eventually called Leonard and was surprised to learn that Tony had moved out. Leonard told me that although he missed Tony, he could understand his decision. He explained that Tony had fallen in love with Michael Ottway,[14] an easy-going young man from Ohio, and that Tony and Michael had decided to move in together. I accepted that news of his relationship wasn't what a twenty-one-year-old was likely to share with his mother, but when I reflected that Tony had probably traded career-commitment and no financial stress for a new lifestyle and a very tight budget, I was disappointed and became very concerned.

Leonard explained that Tony and Michael had searched for somewhere to set up home and had settled on a Lower East Side apartment

---

14 Pseudonym.

on the top floor of a brick tenement with an external zig-zag fire-escape facing the street. Tony had described the apartment as being very compact, with an open living area, small kitchen, smaller bathroom and tiny bedroom. They'd furnished and decorated it and made it cosy, and although I felt happy about his new relationship, I was sadly aware of the risks that accompanied his changed lifestyle. With a fun-loving partner to share his love of music, passion for theatre and enthusiasm for life, and with Manhattan's bathhouses and gay discos on hand to add lustre to their social lives, I accepted that despite having sacrificed the benefits of living with Leonard, Tony would be busy and happy.

I'd heard little about gay bathhouses then, but years later, after reading Larry Kramer's book *Faggots*, I understood their significance and the risks they had posed to the gay community. Following the 1969 Stonewall riots, and with changing attitudes through the 1970s and '80s, gay people could go to bathhouses without fear of harassment, so the popularity of bathhouses had soared.

By the early '80s, bathhouses had become popular places for socialising and hooking up just when the AIDS virus was taking off; for the gay community, what had been hard won was fast becoming a risk to their very existence. Doctors were connecting the rapid escalation of the HIV infection rate with bathhouse activity and, despite the advent of safe sex, were taking steps to have them closed down. New York had several, the more conventional providing traditional saunas and pools, others offering vast menus of sexual entertainment from splash-pools and spas, discos and bars to sex-cubicled corridors, even orgy rooms, with condoms and sex-enhancing drugs as readily available as cocktails and coffee. Those whose interest lay more in socialising could while away their leisure hours in coffee shops, libraries, music rooms or chat rooms. New Yorkers of the eighties weren't prepared to allow AIDS to cramp their style.

* * *

Tony's brother Phil was his first visitor. From the moment Tony and Michael welcomed him at the airport in a hired limousine until they farewelled him, the visit whirled by. Tony took Phil 'out on the town', dropping into bars and discos, eating in tucked-away cafes known only to locals, and proudly showing off 'his' New York City. Phil told me he was pleased to find Tony so exhilarated by his Big-Apple lifestyle, enjoying his work and, best of all, making good progress at Lee Strasberg. On their last day together, sitting in the apartment chatting over breakfast, Phil had told Tony how worried we all were about AIDS. Tony didn't appear too concerned. His response was 'I can't live as though there'll be no tomorrow. We've all got to keep our spirits up because what's happening here is horrendous. I'm being careful but I can't change my lifestyle because of a disease.'

When Phil reported this back to me, I felt perturbed about Tony's cavalier attitude towards AIDS and, recalling his childhood suicide attempt, hoped his death wish no longer lingered.

* * *

In December 1982, Tony had turned twenty-one. For Thanksgiving he'd visited St Louis to spend the holidays with the Stennards, and his newsy letter arrived soon afterwards, just in time for Christmas:

> I'm sitting in the apartment listening to Ravel. The crystal koala you sent for my birthday is sparkling on the coffee table and the mohair rug is hanging over the end of the bed. It's cosy. Thank you. I'm spending many hours learning and rehearsing monologues for auditions. I have two jobs . . . Busy is an understatement. I agree with another student that 'being an actor in New York City is probably the most difficult life someone could choose for themselves – we must all be crazy . . .' Just bumped into my old school friend Scott Whitmont. You'll remember Scott – he was our neighbour and we used to take the train to

school together. He's recently arrived in town to visit his sister Steph ... Merry Christmas, Ho, Ho, Ho, HAPPY NEW YEAR (balloons and streamers), Tony-oni-Macaroni.

* * *

In mid-1984, one of the most high-profile AIDS-related deaths in Australia occurred: Bobby Goldsmith, a gay Australian champion swimmer, died aged thirty-eight. He'd won 17 medals in swimming in 1982 at the first Gay Olympics, and I was alarmed at how quickly the disease had taken its toll. Sydneysiders were in shock.

Then the best news of the year was hailed worldwide: the AIDS virus had at last been discovered, simultaneously by both American and French researchers. Despite this, widespread fear and discrimination continued, along with the appalling treatment meted out to people with AIDS.

The battle lines were being drawn.

* * *

The flow of letters and cards from Tony kept me updated about his work, acting, singing classes and auditions. There was never a mention of either Michael or of AIDS.

From his choice of artwork on his card, I was able to read his mood, even before I read his words. A sunny New York crowded street scene on brown paper with writing in silver ink conveyed carefree confidence:

> Singing classes with Renata going very well, have developed my voice to two-and-a-half octaves ... Yesterday your fruit cake arrived – best cake you've made, very moist and fresh ... Thank you for help with tuition fees ... Organising an agent and photos, rehearsing monologues for auditions ...

Met Dizzy Gillespie . . . Working part-time at Fourth Street
Card, a specialty stationery shop . . .

A few months later an Ansel Adams black-and-white photograph of rolling pastures and grey-blotched clouds suggested a more pensive mood, reinforced by his words:

> Last few months have been bloody awful. Trying to sort out a lot of problems, not only personal but getting off doing drugs and alcohol and partying too much. What I want to do with my life is difficult enough without adding any unnecessary problems . . . I'm enclosing a photograph of me taken especially for you by my friend Vladimir, a photographer formerly with the Russian Ballet.
> With my love to everyone,
> Tony-oni-Macaroni

His candour about drugs surprised me. I had no idea what drugs he was referring to. Marijuana? Cocaine? I'd read that both were popular and freely available in New York so I was relieved that thankfully, whatever it had been, he'd put it behind him. A few weeks later a reverse-charge phone call revealed his reformation had proved rewarding:
'Guess what? I've made it into the '84 season of Shakespeare in the Park. We'll be doing *Henry V* at the Delacorte Theater in Central Park, and I'm playing the part of Louis, Dauphin of France. He's a great character – a rather cocky brat who's pretty rude to good old King Henry and if I play it well, it's sure to lead to bigger things.'
It did. In early 1985 he was invited to direct two short plays at Central Park's Cottage Theater. Then came the jackpot: he landed the lead role of Dr Frankenstein in an off-Broadway production *Frankenstein: New Wave*, a Denis Woychuk production. His star was rising.

Children and Art

* * *

In October 1985, I boarded an Amtrak train at Union Station, Los Angeles, bound for New York City. As I rested against the clear dome of the viewing car, vast golden cornfields dotted with mansard-roofed barns floated past and residents of small towns nodded and waved when we slowed at road crossings. Imaginary river songs echoed to the rhythm of the mighty Mississippi as it rolled beneath the steel bridge that led us into St Louis. We continued on to Chicago, to pause awhile before we clickety-clacked towards the East Coast, and plunged beneath the Hudson River to re-emerge at New York's Grand Central Station.

A beaming Tony waited on the platform. 'That is the only way to come into New York City, Lezzles, up from the bowels of the earth,' he proclaimed, a grin as broad as the Hudson lighting his face.

I stepped out into a kaleidoscope of colour, chaotic movement, exotic aromas and the cacophony of sound that is New York City. Pedestrians dodged and wove through bumper-to-bumper traffic as my introduction to this amazing metropolis confirmed what Tony had meant: by comparison Sydney seemed practically deserted.

Before heading off to stay with Tony's friend Jo-Anne in Greenwich Village, we called in at his apartment. By the time we'd climbed to the fifth floor, I was relieved I'd travelled light. He ushered me in. It wasn't the 'cosy' place he'd described a year earlier. The furniture was sparse. It felt lonely. When he went to make coffee his admission that the 'last few months have been bloody awful' suddenly added up: he and Michael must have parted.

We caught up on three years' worth of what letters and calls couldn't cover. We talked of Tilly, gazing through tears at a photo of our loyal friend's final resting-place beneath a flowering crabapple tree in our garden.

Behind Tony's cheerfulness lay a pale weariness. In between his two jobs he grabbed as much rest as he could, but it seemed to me that it might not be enough. Despite this, Dr Frankenstein came to life every night, his sinister voice, evil eyes and macabre make-up creating the menacing split character that Tony revelled in portraying. On the three occasions I attended, every seat in the off-Broadway in-the-round theatre was occupied and the audiences were rapt.

Greenwich Village's arty ambience was infectious. Its stylish shops – florists, bookshops, bars and cafes – all presenting their wares on tree-lined sidewalks. Many cafes promoted a healthy lifestyle by offering organic foods and their own herbal tonic: 'Boost your immune system with a wheatgrass shot – $3 a shot', the chalkboards proclaimed. Tony stopped by a café every morning after breakfast to join a queue of young men lining up for their daily dark-green 'shots', served in liqueur glasses. I saw how desperate these men were to maximise their good health by whatever means they could in the shadow of HIV/AIDS. Keeping their immune systems fortified was taking priority over more indulgent pleasures.

Locals greeted me with a smile or a wave, a 'Hi there' or 'Good morning', as I ambled through the village each morning to our regular breakfast rendezvous. I soon learned tips for walking safely around the streets of the city: wear plain apparel, worn joggers and no jewellery, carry no handbag, keep your wallet out of sight, walk tall and look confident. I explored the lanes and the backstreets, into Fifth Avenue and through Central Park, while Tony worked and took classes.

One day, at Tony's urging, I bought tickets for *Sunday in the Park with George*, a musical about the French impressionist painter Georges Seurat.

'Sondheim's a genius,' Tony told me, 'and there's a song at the end you'll love.'

In the closing lyric 'Children and Art', George's aging mother Marie reflects on her life: 'There are only two worthwhile things we leave behind when we're gone,' she sings, 'our children and our art.'

Tony gave my hand a squeeze and at that moment the chasm ceased to exist.

* * *

Some nights we dined at Greenwich Village Trattoria, the Italian restaurant where Tony worked as a part-time waiter and where I met some of his many friends, whom I'd join to chat late into the night. After dinner one night, Tony sprang a surprise: 'Quentin Crisp and Robert Patrick would like to meet you, so I've arranged for us to have dinner with them on Tuesday.'

To Tony, Quentin Crisp was the original gay activist, an early pioneer against discrimination, and as such he'd earned hero status in Tony's eyes. They'd become good friends. Robert Patrick was equally well known.

'Robert's a playwright and his play, *Kennedy's Children*, was on Broadway some years ago,' Tony explained. 'It's about what happened here in the sixties during the Kennedy presidency so you wouldn't have heard much about it in Australia and you probably never will, but it was certainly a big hit over here in its day. It's a great play.' Getting to know New York's theatrical literati was one of the plusses of waitering at theatrical events and studying at Lee Strasberg. There was warmth amongst them, a friendly acceptance of their fellow enthusiasts. The week before, as we walked towards the Metropolitan Museum of Art, Tony had stopped to chat with a curly haired, sprightly young man, clad casually in shorts, navy singlet and sandals, who wheeled around to greet him: 'Hi Tony, great to see you. *Frankenstein New Wave* seems to be going well. I hear it's getting some pretty good reviews, too. Well done! I'll be there on Thursday night, so we'll catch up then. See you after the show.'

'That's great. I'll look forward to it,' Tony replied, turning to introduce me. 'James, this is my mother, Lesley. She's here on a visit.'

He filled me in later. 'James and his friend Jerry Ragni wrote *Hair*.'

* * *

After-theatre dinners are of necessity late, so it was eleven thirty when Robert and Quentin approached us from the Broadway theatre where they'd just seen *Cats*. What a stage-worthy double act they were: Robert, head and shoulders taller than Quentin, with neatly trimmed moustache, goatee and wavy hair, greying at the temples, elegant in black skivvy and high-collared dark coat, oozing sophistication; Quentin, colourful in an apricot shirt and tangerine paisley cravat, bobbing alongside in graceful gait, a jaunty black fedora framing his upswept silver hair, rouged cheeks and mascara'd lashes.

An ornate wooden staircase led us into a dimly lit basement restaurant. A waiter ushered us to a white-clothed round table, took Robert's coat and waited for Quentin to remove his hat. He didn't. Instead he offered me his hand and greeted me with a benevolent smile that endowed him with the grace of a kindly maiden aunt.

'Welcome to New York. I hope you'll find her just as welcoming as I've done,' he purred, his accentless elocution perfect. 'New Yorkers are very friendly, and completely accepting. You could walk down Fifth Avenue with a poached egg on your head and no-one would take the least bit of notice.'

I warmed to him immediately.

Robert and Quentin were on a high. *Cats* had received thunderous applause and a standing ovation, so we clinked glasses and wished it a long season on Broadway. The three men's repartee, as witty and entertaining as any Broadway script, set the pace for a jolly evening as we laughed over their tales of life in the Big Apple and they quizzed me about Sydney and theatre Down Under, eager to know whether our opera house was living up to its promise. We compared Australian and American wines, then, pleasantly relaxed, settled into more serious conversation that inevitably turned to politics and the epidemic.

Shortly before my visit, Hollywood star Rock Hudson had died of AIDS. The three men were emotional, and I realised how deeply the epidemic was affecting them.

'Rock was a close friend of Ronald and Nancy Reagan,' said Robert.

'The Reagans were rather proud of the friendship. It gave them political clout and plenty of positive publicity, so now Reagan's in a bit of tight spot after his heartless attitude to AIDS sufferers. Well, now it's our turn to gloat. Rock's death might be just the twist of fate that will force Reagan to finally take AIDS seriously.'

All Americans loved the six-foot-four actor whose gentle eyes and sexy smile had brought an entire generation of American women to swooning-point. I'd read about Rock's trip to Paris three months earlier to receive treatment for AIDS, whereby he had unwittingly brought the epidemic into the public arena. Now that their star had died from an AIDS-related illness, Americans were stunned.

'Let's hope Rock Hudson's death will show just how despicably Reagan's government has abandoned the gay community here,' Tony asserted.

'Did you know that he bequeathed a $250,000 legacy to fund AIDS research?' added Robert. 'That should highlight the way Reagan's government has made beggars out of our medical researchers by denying them funding.'

'Here's to you, Rock.'

We raised our glasses and toasted Rock Hudson and his generous legacy.

'I used to think that AIDS was nothing more than a fad,' mused Quentin. 'I didn't realise how bad it would become.'

'Well, Australia's new government looks set to do a better job than America's,' Tony boasted. 'So, maybe, if or when AIDS takes off over there, things might be different. The new Minister for Health, Dr Neal Blewett, has already taken the bull by the horns. He's calmed down calls to quarantine everyone with HIV, and to mass-test all gay men. Can you believe they were really considering that? In fact, Blewett's already established an AIDS task force and he's allocated research funding as well, even before an epidemic gets going.'

I was impressed to hear that Tony had been keeping his eye on Australia's AIDS politics.

'I think I must pay Australia a visit, perhaps one day quite soon,' Quentin proposed, with a smile.

* * *

On my last morning in New York we set off early for a mystery destination.

We walked in the crisp early-morning air till we reached Fifth Avenue, Tony stopping at a kiosk along the way to pick up takeaway coffees and bagels in brown paper bags.

'We've arrived,' he announced.

Feasting our eyes on displays of sparkling gems and glass sculptures, we ate our breakfast at Tiffany's.

That night I returned for one last performance of *Frankenstein New Wave*. From the opening night, audiences had been enthusiastic. Not only did the show survive its potentially devastating new show reviews, but it ran for a further three weeks. With tears in my eyes, I applauded not only the star's performance but his success in having made it there.

In November 1982, Professor Ron Penny, an immunologist at St Vincent's Hospital, diagnosed the first case of AIDS in Australia.

It took him nearly a month to be sure. The patient, a 27-year-old New York City resident who was visiting Sydney on a working holiday, was referred to the hospital suffering respiratory distress and likely pneumonia.

He was a gay man who averaged six new sexual contacts a month, frequently inhaled amyl nitrate (poppers) during sexual activity and had previously been exposed to a range of sexually transmitted infections such as Hepatitis A and B, herpes and amoebiasis (intestinal disease).

He thus presented with many of the risk factors for AIDS, however, and in the absence of a diagnostic test it took numerous telephone conversations with experts at the United States Center for Disease Control for them to be convinced.

None of the doctors could have suspected the effects that AIDS would have on their lives and the nature of their work in the coming decade.

Paul Sendziuk, *Learning to Trust: Australian responses to AIDS*

Tony with friends at his farewell party
before returning to Australia, Manhattan, 1986.

Chapter 10

Call to Arms

> Tony's New York stardom didn't happen but little did I know he was about to take on the role of his life.
>
> Simon Hunt, 1995

1986

Soon after my return to Australia, tragedy struck. Stuart Morson died.

Andrew and Elizabeth were in disbelief, and the medical fraternity of Royal Prince Alfred Hospital was shocked and deeply saddened at the sudden loss of their leading neurosurgeon.

What had begun as a normal day changed their lives forever. Stuart, capped, gloved and gowned, scalpel in hand, suddenly hunched over his patient and dropped to the floor in the operating theatre. A shaky assistant surgeon took over the brain surgery while nurses and a junior doctor rushed to Stuart's aid. He'd had a heart attack and never regained consciousness. He was sixty-four.

Tony loved Stuart. He'd been a generous friend and mentor, and Elizabeth was like a second mother. The suddenness of the tragedy weighed heavily on the family, drawing them close in their grief. Andrew called Tony, their conversation more sobs and tears than words. Andrew and George moved to Karingal to stay with Elizabeth. As Elizabeth came to terms with widowhood, Tony regularly phoned her, and she drew comfort from his overseas calls.

To help overcome his sadness, Andrew decided to visit Tony. He'd missed the easy closeness of their friendship and the special bond they'd formed as little boys in prep school.

'We haven't seen each other for three years now,' Andrew told me. 'I have quite a surprise in store for him.'

Excitement bubbled in his voice as he described his plans for a theatrical entrance into the Big Apple: 'It's all arranged. Tony will be there waiting. He'll be expecting me to walk up, and I can just imagine the look on his face when a helicopter drops down out of the sky and I jump out.'

We both chuckled and I wished him a happy trip, picturing Tony's reaction to Andrew's arrival through the skyscrapers.

* * *

'Lesley,' said the familiar voice, 'I hope you're sitting down because I have bad news.'

It was Andrew again, so I assumed he was calling from New York, but the telltale delays of long-distance calls were missing. Something wasn't right.

'I'm gay and I've got AIDS.'

The first part of his double bombshell didn't surprise. But AIDS? How could that be possible? Andrew's lifestyle wasn't risky. Perhaps the AIDS part was simply a mistake, a misdiagnosis. Sounding as though he was finding it difficult to hold back tears, Andrew told me what had happened:

'I never made it to New York,' he explained softly. 'Elizabeth had to come to Los Angeles to bring me home.'

Exhilarated by the prospect of seeing Tony, Andrew had ignored his niggling cough and boarded the plane for Los Angeles. He said he'd felt fine, just a little tired. By the time he'd arrived in Honolulu, he'd become weak and dizzy, and as he continued his journey his cough became relentless and he felt hot and clammy. It had taken the flight attendant just one look to suspect that she had a seriously ill passenger on her hands. A doctor on the plane diagnosed a lung infection and notified the pilot, who arranged to have an ambulance meet the plane when it landed. Andrew was taken directly to Los Angeles General Hospital, and because he was so critically ill, the hospital called Elizabeth.

'We have your son here in our intensive care unit. Andrew's condition is critical and he may not survive the night. He has PCP pneumonia, which means he also has full-blown AIDS. If Andrew survives, he'll be here until he's well enough to fly home. We'd like you to get here as soon as you can.'

I wondered how Andrew could possibly have become infected with HIV: George was his only partner and their relationship was stable. George hadn't visited America for years and Andrew had never been there. Could he have picked it up at the Opera House, perhaps serving food to an infected American visitor? Maybe the disease was passed on by sharing contaminated eating utensils after all. Or even a mosquito bite? Andrew wondered, Elizabeth and I wondered. George wondered whether he'd unwittingly been the conduit. He'd been an airline steward on Qantas's Sydney–San Francisco run in the early days of HIV/AIDS, long before he'd met Andrew. One casual sexual encounter could have passed the virus to him, leaving him unknowingly infectious. Assuming this to be so, George realised that he too could be HIV-positive. A test confirmed his status.

When I told my husband Jim, he was concerned. 'This puts us in a very difficult spot. I'm sure you'll want to support Elizabeth and Andrew, and so do I, but we'll need to be very careful because doctors still don't seem to know much about AIDS. We'd better try to find out how it spreads so we can protect ourselves.'

I had a basic understanding of viruses, and if AIDS was a virus, as was supposed, why didn't frequent handwashing keep it at bay, as it did other germs?

Studying horticulture had taught me that mosquitoes and other blood-sucking insects could pass viruses from plant to plant via sap, so why couldn't mosquitos pass the HIV/AIDS virus from person to person by blood, as they can malaria? And if the cold virus could be transmitted by sharing eating and drinking utensils or through kissing or sneezing, then why not AIDS? Jim and I rang the Department of Health's AIDS hotline for answers as to whether HIV could be transmitted through saliva and tears or mosquitos.

'We don't believe so, but we're still not certain. We just don't know yet. It seems to take a larger volume of bodily fluid than just a drop to pass it on, but we don't understand why,' we were told.

Their replies didn't add up and left us even more confused. So we decided to compromise: we'd give our love and support to Elizabeth and Andrew. How could we not? But at the same time, we'd take every possible care with any behaviour we thought might be risky.

For a few months Andrew was his usual happy self. He lost weight and looked pale but otherwise seemed okay. One day he didn't come to the door to greet us. Instead, he called out from the living room.

'Come in, the door's unlocked.'

He turned and smiled from his chair. 'I'm a bit the worse for wear today. It seems I've become anaemic, so Elizabeth's taking me to hospital tomorrow for a blood transfusion.'

That was all the doctors could offer Andrew despite his plummeting T-cell count.[15]

When we walked into Elizabeth's living room a week later, Andrew was sitting in a floral chintz chair, singing along to 'Memory', from the musical *Cats*. The transfusion had pinked his cheeks but his once-rounded face had prominent cheekbones we'd not noticed before.

'Hi, Lesley and Jim. Have you heard this wonderful music from *Cats*? The songs are really catchy, and cheeky, too. I'm hoping I might somehow get to see it before the season ends.'

---

15 T-cells are part of the immune system that helps protect the body from infection. The AIDS virus destroys T-cells.

I jumped at an opportunity to do something positive. 'I'll get some tickets. It's on at the Theatre Royal. Jim and I will pick you up and drive you there.'

Andrew flashed us a beaming smile.

When we arrived at Karingal to collect Andrew for a Saturday matinee, Elizabeth greeted us at the door, shaking her head. 'I'm afraid Andrew's not feeling too well.'

There were three empty seats at the *Cats* matinee that afternoon. Instead we stayed with Elizabeth and Andrew and learned about alternative therapies: slippery elm for digestive problems; bananas, rice and apple sauce for diarrhoea; yoghurt and cranberry juice for thrush; aloe vera for rashes . . .

After each blood transfusion Andrew's restored energy became more short-lived until he seldom left his bed. Elizabeth remained ever optimistic. She focused on Andrew's 'good' days and trusted the healing power of herbs, but gradually the demands of being a full-time carer began to take their toll. When we visited, it was I who made the tea so that Elizabeth could take a break while Jim chatted with Andrew. An optimistic smile masked her tiredness, but there was a bleak look in her eyes.

Elizabeth was gentle, with a frailty about her, a dreamy romantic whose eyes readily crinkled into a smile. She wore little make-up on her fine skin and often drew her lustrous brown hair into a bun. She quietly accepted whatever came her way with grace but deep down she possessed an inner strength. One morning she answered the telephone to an unfamiliar female voice.

'We've all heard about your son and his filthy disease. You ought to be ashamed. You should have done something about his homosexuality years ago when there was still time to cure him. Now he's brought AIDS here to Castlecrag. Do your shopping somewhere else.'

This was the first of many similarly abusive calls. Elizabeth was experiencing the deeply damaging and hurtful mistreatment and discrimination meted out to families living with AIDS.

Andrew's decline continued. One day he raised the possibility of seeing Tony once more. 'I'd really like to see Tony before I die. I was terribly disappointed about not making it to New York and it would mean so much. Do you think he'd come back home for me?'

I rang Tony that night.

'How did he get so sick so quickly? Andrew shouldn't even have AIDS. He's never been out of Australia. Are they sure?'

'I'm sure they've have tested him for it, so it must be true,' I replied. 'I don't think he's going to last too much longer. If you decide you'd like to come back, even for just a short visit, I'll get you a ticket. Look, Tony, I do understand that right now isn't a good time for you to leave New York, just when your career's taking off, but please think about it because I can see how much it would mean to Andrew.' I hadn't expected what followed.

'I didn't want to worry you about this, Lezzles, but I have a problem with coming home. I don't have a passport anymore. It was stolen two years ago when I was robbed, so now I'm an illegal immigrant. I'm really not too worried because apparently Reagan's about to announce an amnesty for aliens. In fact, it could happen any day, and when it does, I'll automatically get US residency.'

Unlike Andrew, Tony hadn't suggested I sit down to hear his bad news. Had I known about it earlier, I'd not only have woken and worried in the early hours of every morning, as I already did – I'd probably not have slept at all. As an alien in New York City, should some mishap befall him, he'd be unidentifiable.

Yet Tony's longstanding loyalty to Andrew meant he wanted to come home if I could sort out his passport problem. The US consulate in Sydney seemed the place to go, and having Keith on board would surely improve the odds.

When I called Keith, he listened patiently as I explained Tony's predicament. He vehemently blamed Tony for getting into his unenviable passport position, and as for Andrew's illness, I was grateful not to be telling him about it face to face. However, after a short silence, he agreed to help. He suggested I come to Bethungra. 'Connie would love to show you what she's done with this old pub and we can work out how to handle Tony's passport problem together.'

* * *

The grand old satiny-black-granite Shirley Hotel stood proud beside tall, black-trunked gums and blue-green wattles. As we arrived, the upstairs iron-lace balconies caught the fading western sun. Shirley's clients crowded around the bar, good humour abounding in rollicking response to the endless rounds of beers Keith was serving. Jollied by several chardonnays, I borrowed Connie's scissors and gave a haircut to a shaggy farmer in the corner of the bar room who'd complained that his pastoral duties had denied him time to visit the town's lone barber.

Over bacon and eggs in the pub's kitchen the following morning, Keith agreed to meet me at the US consulate in Sydney as soon as an appointment could be made.

* * *

Keith waited on the corner of Elizabeth Street outside the ten-storey grey office-block, occasionally ambling back and forth across the pavement to avoid wind-blown spray from the fountains bordering the garden beds. Wisecracking about the number of police surrounding the building, we scanned the list of occupants to discover that the US consulate was located on the eighth floor.

Two policemen, leashed sniffer dogs at hand, approached us. 'We'd like you to leave this area immediately. We're investigating a bomb scare.'

Renewing Tony's passport had morphed into an obstacle race but having made it this far, I was loath to leave without at least a plea for help:

'We have an urgent appointment with the United States consul so we'd be prepared to take the risk if you'd allow us to take the lift to the eighth floor.'

The two policemen suddenly looked serious and escorted us, guns at the ready and dogs on alert, directly into the consulate's office. We pleaded our case as distraught Australian parents and by the time we left, the consul's secretary had arranged for Tony's new passport to be available from New York Customs in five days, with no impediment to him being allowed to return to the US.

'We've just been informed that the bomb scare was a hoax, Madam,' a grinning police officer informed us as we hurried from the scene.

* * *

> I knew exactly what it would be like when I came back from the States for my friend who was dying. At the end, I was the only one there apart from his lover and his mum. We even had doctors who refused to come to the house.
>
> Tony's journal, 1995

Though sad to be turning his back on his budding career and hopes of US residency, Tony returned to Australia. As he sat by Andrew's bedside in the room where they'd shared so many schoolboy secrets, he accepted that his friend was already lost. Gazing into Andrew's sunken eyes, Tony came face to face for the first time with the agony of AIDS. He'd seen it in New York, but from a distance. This time was different. It was someone he loved.

He joined former school friends Roy, Rajah and Jeremy, who had rallied to provide round-the-clock care for Andrew. The former Pennryn schoolboys, now men, drew up a roster so they could juggle home lives, study and jobs with their new roles as carers. Tony was ready and willing to help, despite the urgency of needing to arrange somewhere to live and find part-time work. Both fell very conveniently into place: 'You can move into our spare room at Avalon,' Phil offered. 'There's a double-bed futon there and Jenny and I would really enjoy your company.'

Fortuitously, Michael and Judy McMahon, the owners of Barrenjoey House, Palm Beach's historic former inn, now a restaurant, were seeking an experienced waiter. Applicants were scarce because waiters seldom ventured to places like Palm Beach, on Sydney's Northern Beaches, over an hour's drive from the city, so when a silver-service waiter with wine knowledge knocked on their door, they couldn't believe their luck.

'Well done, mate, that's fantastic,' said Phil. 'Barrenjoey House is only a stone's throw from our house. You can walk there or even borrow my bike and ride if you like. And whatever time you've got left after helping Andrew, we can spend sailboarding.'

Andrew's band of carers persuaded Elizabeth to return to Tuesday tennis and did their best to lift Karingal's melancholy air. Andrew's doctor versed them in donning surgical gloves, managing body fluids, avoiding mosquitoes and taking no risks as they took turns in dealing with an illness that was not yet understood.

The brutal reality of fear and discrimination was never far away. A coffin was pre-delivered to Karingal and left in the spare room. Undertakers refused to handle the bodies of those who'd died of AIDS, so Elizabeth was left with instructions that Andrew's body was to be placed into the coffin, the lid glued down, then nailed shut.

The end came softly and silently during the night. With Elizabeth, Tony and George by his side, Andrew's life ebbed gently away like the final flicker of a candle as the wick sinks into its pool of melted wax.

The next morning Elizabeth, Tony and George bathed and dressed Andrew, laid him in his coffin, and followed the undertaker's directions.

Somewhere in a forgotten drawer, Elizabeth discovered a poem Tony had written when he and Andrew were eleven-year-old boys from prep school. She asked Tony to read it at Andrew's memorial service:

> Happiness starts with love and peace, Happiness comes through friends you please,
> Happiness means to share and give, Happiness is something that always lives,
> Happiness hugs with a laugh and a tickle, Happiness grows like the shrill of a whistle,
> Happiness goes then comes back again, Happiness is Andrew, a life-long friend.

As we drove back to Elizabeth's house, a Cape chestnut tree, its branches laden with pink blossoms, caught Tony's eye. 'What's that beautiful tree?' he asked. 'I'd like to plant one of those for Andrew in Elizabeth's back garden, where we used to play.'

The tree lives to this day, spreading its shady branches and dropping a pink spring carpet in the corner of a bushland garden where the spirits of two boys roam free.

AIDS Girl Eve Dies

Eve van Grafhorst, the little AIDS girl who fled Australia in 1986 with her family when she was banned from going to pre-school, died peacefully in her mother's arms yesterday.

The eleven-year-old who captured hearts around the world by her bravery was surrounded by family and friends at their home in Hawkes Bay, New Zealand.

Eve was the first child in Australia to contract AIDS via a blood transfusion.

She got national attention when, as a spry two-year-old, she was thrown out of pre-school in Kincumber, near Gosford NSW, by a scared local council when she tested HIV-positive.

Her mother was 29 weeks into her pregnancy when she had an emergency caesarean delivery.

No-one was aware the blood transfusion which had saved Eve was HIV-positive. That would only emerge two-and-a-half years later.

The Sydney Morning Herald, 21 November 1993

From left to right: Lynna, Jane holding baby Ben, Tony and Phil, Avalon, 1986.

Chapter 11

'I Don't Want to Talk About It'

> When I was first diagnosed HIV positive, the news was so terrifying I chose to ignore it. Two years later I changed my mind. Basically I realised that I must take responsibility for my situation if I am to live on and survive.
>
> Tony's journal, 1995

1987

Tony remained at Karingal with Elizabeth for a few weeks. She recalled years later how much it had meant to her that he was there when Andrew's loss was so raw and how on his days off they'd wander around the garden reminiscing about the Pennryn years and the fun he and Andrew had had as budding cinematographers using Stuart's movie camera.

George, having told his parents about his HIV status, returned to Perth.

'I wasn't too sure at first how my parents would take it because it came as a quite a shock,' George had told me. 'But after they'd had time to think about it, they invited me to come back home.'

When he died two years later, Elizabeth grieved not only for George but for another mother's loss. As was the unpredictable course of HIV, George's immune system had afforded him many more years of life than had Andrew's.

* * *

An electric storm lashed the night sky, its lightning spears illuminating Pittwater. In brief flashes, Barrenjoey House lit up then disappeared. It had been deserted since Judy and Michael had left Palm Beach to open their new restaurant, Bilsons on Circular Quay, and Tony had moved with them. There was still no indication he was thinking of returning to New York so I waited and wondered, but asked no questions.

'It's been wonderful staying here with you two,' Tony had told Jenny and Phil, 'but now that I'm working in the city it's just too far to commute. Luckily, I've found a share flat in Bondi.'

So Phil and Tony exchanged their time together sailboarding with catching up on Tuesday afternoons in a Darlinghurst bar.

By this time, Jim and I had been living in Avalon for several years. We'd found our dream house, perched on a hillside overlooking the sprawling waters of Pittwater, which open out into Broken Bay near the mouth of the Hawkesbury River. It was liberating to be an empty-nester, whose children had 'flown the coop'. Lynna, her partner Doug, and their dog Kiri the boxer lived two beaches away, and Jane and her husband Christopher lived in Queensland.

Soon after Tony returned to Australia, he'd stood looking out over Careel Bay towards Lion Island and told me, 'This must be one of the most beautiful places in Australia – in the world, even. I can understand why you want to live here. It might be a long way from the city, but for all this peace and beauty, it's well worthwhile.'

Although he had a special place in his heart for the throb of a big city, he also appreciated Pittwater's bays, beaches and rugged sandstone headlands. Perhaps he'd heard her songs, as I had. She sang of birds and breezes in spotted gums, of steel halliards jangling and tinkling against masts, of leisure sailboats bobbing on the green waters of the bay. Our life there was about as good as it could get.

One sunny Saturday morning she beckoned us.

'Pittwater's looking fairly calm today, and there's a good breeze out there so let's pack some lunch and sail up to Kincumber,' suggested Jim.

But the phone's shrill ring interrupted my dreamy anticipation of this outing. I sprang out of bed and pattered down the hall, the slate floor cold under my feet. Glancing at my watch, I focused my mind. *Seven-thirty? Too early for a social call.*

'It's Michael McMahon here, Lesley. I'm sorry to call you so early but I'm worried about Tony. Do you know where he is?'

'He should be at home in Bondi right now, sleeping in,' I replied. 'He worked last night, didn't he?'

'He hasn't been at work for three days now. That's just not like Tony, you and I both know that. I'm concerned, in fact very much so.'

'That's odd. He rang me last Monday and he seemed fine. He was excited about an audition he had coming up,' I said, almost as much to reassure myself, but I felt apprehensive. 'I'll try to find him, Michael, and I'll keep you posted.'

I eased the phone back into its cradle. The doors onto the deck were open and the sun was streaming in, so I wandered out and stared down at the bay, looking for answers. Jim appeared, carrying two mugs of steaming coffee.

'What's happened, Lezzles?'

His comforting arms were warm around me. I sank into his chest. 'Tony's missing,' I whispered.

The morning wore on. Angst turned to action. I trembled as we summed up the situation and considered the possibilities. Tony had been missing for three days. During that time we'd heard nothing, not from him, or his friends, or a hospital, or the police. If he'd had an accident, he'd surely have been found by now. What could have caused him to disappear? Was he okay? Where was he? He lived in an apartment near the beach at Bondi with flatmates Garth and Steve. He travelled to work by bus or, if he was running short of time, a taxi. When Bilson's closed, often quite late, he and at least one other staff member would lock up together then share a taxi home. When he visited either us or Elizabeth he always took public transport, which was straightforward and safe. No loopholes there. He sometimes rode his bicycle to the beach to run on the sand or swim in the surf, so that might bear looking into. We decided we'd begin by calling Tony's flatmates.

Garth and Steve were as nonplussed as we were. 'We thought he'd gone to stay with you or Elizabeth, but he usually tells us when he's not coming home, so we're worried too,' Steve said.

'Do you remember when you last saw him?'

'Now I think about it, it was rather strange. He was sitting at the table eating his breakfast on Wednesday morning when the phone rang. He answered it, then put it down, pretty hard in fact, and just got up and walked out. He got on his bike, rode off, and hasn't been back since. It was weird, not like Tony at all.'

'What was he wearing?'

'Just shorts and a t-shirt and his joggers, I think. Look, I'm sorry, but I didn't take too much notice so I can't remember much more than that.'

'Did he take anything with him?'

'Not that I noticed. It all happened so quickly, I thought he was probably just riding to the shops to get some milk and he'd only be gone a few minutes. Then later when he didn't come home we supposed he'd left to see you. But he wouldn't take his bike to do that, would he? That's what puzzled us.'

It was over a week since Lynna had heard from him, and the last Phil had seen of him was on Tuesday when they'd met in the city for a drink. After that, Phil had gone home and Tony to work. Phil's recollection, similar to mine, was that the audition Tony had been anticipating had gone quite well and he seemed okay.

'Mum, I think you'd better get over to Bondi to see what you can find out,' Phil suggested. 'We'd better ring around the hospitals, too, in case he's had an accident. I'll come straight over to help you.'

It was late afternoon when Phil drove us to Bondi. Steve and Garth showed us into Tony's room. The bed was rumpled where he'd slept, his keys were on the bedside table, wallet and passport in the bedside drawer, his waiter's uniform draped over a chair. Garth, Steve and Phil then went through Tony's phone list, calling his contacts to ask if any of them had heard from Tony, but none had. We returned to Avalon, went to the police station and registered Tony as a missing person. As I filled in the coldly bureaucratic form with shaking hand, I pitied every other mother who'd done this before me.

Because sons don't always share details of their private lives with their mothers, I often noted any seemingly unimportant titbits of information Tony would occasionally drop. One such morsel was the name of the doctor he'd visited shortly after he'd moved to Bondi, Dr Brad Harrison.[16] I called Dr Harrison's Darlinghurst surgery and made an appointment to see him later in the day.

'I'm the mother of one of your patients, Tony Carden,' I told him.

'Yes, Mrs Carden, I know Tony. Your son's a very amenable young man.'

'I'm aware of patient–doctor confidentiality, Dr Harrison, but I'm worried about my son and there's something I'd like you to know because he probably wouldn't have mentioned it. Tony has a family, and we love him very much. If he has a problem, we'll always be there to stand by him.'

'Well,' he replied, 'at least you didn't come storming in here like your son Phil did this morning, demanding to know if his brother is HIV positive or not.'

Despite momentary embarrassment at Phil's confronting approach, I appreciated his concern.

---

16 Pseudonym.

The days had dragged by, and it was now a week since Tony had gone missing. My nights were sleepless, thoughts of the burdens Tony already carried haunting me. What had happened at Pennryn to hurt him so badly he couldn't talk about it? Why act as though there was no-one to share 'it' with? How unfortunate that his father found it so difficult to come to terms with having a gay son. With a heavy heart I dreaded the likelihood of a new problem.

On Thursday morning the phone rang. 'Hi, Lezzles. It's Tony-ony-Macaroni here.'

I exploded. 'Where on earth have you been? Do you know how worried we've all been? Whatever happened to you?'

Silence, then: 'I don't want to talk about it.'

His classic answer! I'd heard it before, hadn't I? It was his polite way of saying, 'Mind your own business. Matter closed.'

Suspecting his new problem could be AIDS, I was filled with dread at what might lie ahead.

* * *

Following those tortuous days, my suspicions remained unspoken. Tony mentioned neither the phone call nor his absence. He behaved as though nothing had happened, assuming we'd do likewise. He resumed his role at Bilsons, and Judy and Michael graciously allowed the matter to rest. Norma Bennett, the casting agent he'd engaged shortly after his return from New York, soon filled his non-Bilson's hours.

'I've just landed a couple of jolly good roles,' Tony announced one afternoon. 'The Department of Education has signed me up to make a series of voice-over tapes for teaching history to use in secondary schools. Have you heard of Thomas Mort?'

I recalled the name from long-gone school days.

'Well, next Thursday I'll be Thomas, telling his life story and how he promoted Australian agriculture. Then the following week I'll be William Wentworth crossing the Blue Mountains. It's to bring a more personal touch to teaching history. After all, the way it was taught to us was rather boring. Oh! And as well as that, I've been cast in the remake of a film *The Love Letters from Teralba Road*. It'll be filmed as a TV series and we'll be starting work on that in a couple of months.'

His focus on his theatre career was refreshingly optimistic.

* * *

In April 1987 we met the grim reaper. Never again would any Australian be able to turn a blind eye to AIDS. We were confronted every night for three weeks, at prime viewing time, with the reality of the growing epidemic: in a foggy bowling alley, to the ominous background tolling of a bell, the hooded grim reaper, scythe in one hand, black bowling ball in the other, indiscriminately knocked down men, women, teenagers, children and babies like bowling pins as his grisly voice warned of the likelihood of a death toll in Australia higher than that of World War II should we not heed his warning:

'If you have sex, have just one safe partner or ALWAYS use a condom. ALWAYS.'

The safe-sex message was short, succinct, extremely confronting, but most importantly, successful. It undoubtedly changed the sexual practices of many people, including heterosexuals, most of whom had previously considered themselves safe. The campaign was credited with reducing HIV infection rates, but Tony was concerned by a different aspect of the ad. 'Think of how it portrays the gay community,' he lamented. 'Every gay man will now be identified with the grim reaper and that will alienate them even further.'

He guessed right. The media reported that discrimination towards gay men had increased significantly after the ad was aired and that many young children were having nightmares.

1988

In August Tony announced he was off to Tasmania with a few friends. We wished him well and pictured them exploring Hobart and Launceston, perhaps hiring bicycles to visit remote beaches. A postcard depicting Wineglass Bay bore the message that despite the surf's iciness, it was exhilarating.

What he didn't mention was that he'd had a secret mission: to attend Australia's Third National Conference on AIDS, where, in a world hungry for answers about the deadly virus, the latest in medical and scientific research would be aired.

The Hon. Justice Michael Kirby in his presentation 'AIDS: Insights from the Stockholm Conference' revealed news that must have sent ripples of relief throughout the audience: 'If mosquitoes, toilet seats, sneezing, motherly love, shared utensils or the man who mixes salad at the deli were vectors for AIDS we'd surely have heard by now.'

Such news would certainly have eased my mind.

It emerged later, from others who had attended, that quite a few people attending the conference, including Tony, had worn badges proclaiming themselves 'Alive and Visible'. This was Tony's first public admission about being HIV positive. The number of badges had grown dramatically and rapidly over the four days of the conference, and by the closing ceremony the number of delegates self-identifying as having the virus was overwhelming. At some point during that final session they came forward, Tony merging with the throng, as they claimed the stage for themselves in an act that provoked uproar. Their message was loud and clear: 'Talk TO us, not ABOUT us!'

They'd taken a significant stand, which would result in Australia becoming a world leader in reducing the infection rate of HIV/AIDS.

Australian AIDS activism had begun, and Tony was part of it from its very beginning. On his return he assured us he'd surfed and rested and had a good time, which his tanned face confirmed, but he didn't mention the conference.

Whenever we shopped for the organic fruit, vegies and chicken Tony requested I have on hand whenever he visited, or admired his dedication to his keep-fit gym regime, we'd brush aside our unspoken fears. The months flew by – he worked, auditioned and rehearsed – and then suddenly another year was gone.

'We'll be having Christmas with Keith and Connie this year – Phil, Jenny and me, that is,' Tony announced.

'Whereabouts?' I asked.

'Well, we're looking forward to seeing their new house at Hyams Beach and you never know, maybe good old Keith's homophobia has mellowed by now.'

'Hmm, here's hoping, but I wouldn't count on it.'

'They're getting us together with Connie's kids, and Connie's son's birthday is the same day as mine so there'll be a good excuse for a double celebration. Michael and Judy have given me the whole week off; pretty generous, considering it's Christmas.'

Tony loved Christmas. He relished its magic, its sparkle, the way people became more extroverted when they relaxed, and probably also because it was his birthday. His and Phil's views of Christmas were quite different. Years after Phil's eight-year-old scepticism had led him to check under beds and on top of cupboards to ensure he'd be on the receiving end of the cricket bat or football he was hoping for, Tony, wide-eyed with the wonder of it all, firmly defended the myth of Santa and made me smile, insisting: 'It's true. Philly! It's true! It's the spirit of Saint Nicholas that makes it all happen, so don't you go spoiling it. His spirit makes the presents come and it doesn't really matter how it happens.'

* * *

Jim and I, our car loaded with bicycles, presents and a coin-laden Christmas pudding, set off to join Jane, Chris and their children, four-year-old Ben, two-year-old Daniel and my mother Mary, now 80 and affectionately known as 'Great', for a Wagga Wagga country Christmas.

At first light on Christmas morning, the two little boys tip-toed to the Christmas tree to discover Santa's mysterious overnight delivery, with us close on their heels, not wanting to miss the magic moment. But Jim's usual spark of enthusiasm was missing. His silent disinterest radiated a 'bah, humbug' mood, which was not like Jim at all. When I asked if he was okay, he nodded his head and smiled assurance, but by Boxing Day it was clear he was ill. He had nicked his hand on the edge of the pool, but the small cut wouldn't stop bleeding. He became feverish, developed a sore throat and felt listless, so we moved to a nearby motel where he could rest undisturbed.

The next morning, we went to Wagga Wagga Hospital's busy emergency department. A weary-looking doctor examined Jim, took some blood, and X-rayed his chest. A little later he called us back. 'Mr Saddington, your chest X-ray shows some abnormal shadows and your red blood cell count is extremely low. It could be something serious, but we can't carry out the tests you need here because for the next few days we'll have only a skeleton staff on duty. You should get back to Sydney as quickly as you can. Which hospital would you prefer to go to?'

We gave each other an aching glance and nominated Royal North Shore, the closest major hospital to Avalon. The doctor told us he'd advise them we were on our way. The trip home was traumatic, Jim so pale and listless I feared he may not make it.

Jim's diagnosis was aplastic anaemia – essentially, his body had stopped producing new blood cells. He was placed in an isolation ward, complete with floppy plastic screen doors to keep out germs and suspected germ-carriers. For ten days he struggled, as desperate doctors dug into their arsenal of drugs, until in the early hours of the following Sunday morning Jim's battle was lost.

It was like being hit by an express train. Life became a hazy blur, like something I was seeing from a distance. Grasping for a lifeline, I phoned our local doctor, who'd seen Jim only days earlier, hoping he'd provide a pill to knock me out until I could comprehend this sudden shock.

'Jim died early this morning,' I told him, wondering, as I heard my own words, how they could possibly be true. 'Please Doctor Graaf, can you help me?'

Two hours later he was sitting beside me on our couch. He, too, was shocked by the speed and severity of Jim's decline. He talked about Jim's illness, about the impact of losing a partner suddenly and about the pathway through grief. But he didn't produce the hoped-for knockout pill.

'Just continue doing the things you and Jim enjoyed doing together, the hobbies you had, the activities you shared, like bushwalking, and working in your beautiful garden. Some things you'll decide you never want to do again; others you'll continue to enjoy on your own or perhaps even with other people. Find some new interests, things you haven't done before. Oh, and accept every invitation that comes your way, even though you may prefer otherwise.'

He wrote a name on a sheet of paper and handed it to me. 'Here's the name of a grief counsellor. She's good, and I think you'll find she'll be very helpful.'

In stops and starts I followed Dr Graaf's advice, drank buckets of chamomile tea, lamented the absence of knockout pills and somehow survived the next few days.

Within hours of hearing the news, Jane and Chris arrived with their two little boys in tow and lots of love to tide us over the hollow week ahead. Gradually the house transformed into a fragrant floral forest. Well-wishers appeared then disappeared. Tears fell, arms held me, then suddenly, I was alone.

A late-night knock on the door revealed Tony, smiling, his blue suitcase by his side.

'I'm moving in to stay with you, Lezzles, and I'll stay for as long as it takes. I've told Steve to find another flatmate, so there's no hurry. You'll need someone to keep you company, so here I am.'

His hug was warm and oh-so welcome.

In August 1990 Zidovudine (AZT), a failed cancer drug first approved in US in 1987, is approved in Australia for treatment of people with HIV who have the clinical diagnosis of having less than 500 T-cells, ending the quota system.

The Albion Centre, *A HIV/AIDS Timeline*

Chapter 12

Purple Presage

> Our friendship was liberating because I had young children and to have someone outside the family who was just my friend . . . I'll never forget those perfect eyebrows and that wicked laugh. He was quite exotic in a way. He told us about the scene in America and about the AIDS epidemic. Tony just wanted to live his life, not worry about it.
>
> Judy McMahon, Manager, Catalina Restaurant, 2014

1990

One morning we were breakfasting on the deck, listening to Maria Callas singing *Tosca* from one of Tony's favourite tapes as we guarded our bacon from the kookaburras.

'I've discovered a purple lump on my leg, Lezzles. Would you mind taking a look at it? Maybe you'll have an idea what it is. After all, you did spend a few years working in pathology.'

He chuckled because my 'ancient' pathology career at Sydney Hospital after I'd left school had become a joke between us. The words 'purple lump' gave me goosebumps because, although I'd never seen Kaposi sarcoma, I'd read about it in the tidbits about AIDS that occasionally surfaced in the papers.

'Show me.'

He rolled up his jeans and there it was, on his shin: a raised purple bruise about a centimetre wide. There was only one way to be certain about a lesion and that was to biopsy it, so I suggested we visit Dr Graaf. 'He'll probably arrange for you to have it removed and have pathology done on it.'

We sat there on the deck looking out over the bay, each deep in our own thoughts as the kookaburras stole our bacon.

We were referred to a skin surgeon to have the lesion removed. After Tony was wheeled back to his room, we waited for the surgeon's diagnosis, making small talk to avoid thinking about our apprehension.

'I'm so sorry to have to tell you this,' the surgeon began, gently, 'but Tony's lesion is Kaposi sarcoma, which means he's probably been HIV-positive for a few years and now it's progressed to full-blown AIDS.'

We asked no questions. I just put my arms around him, and we both wept as we gazed out the window to the ocean and the hazy horizon.

'Let's keep this between just you and me please, Lezzles. I don't want anyone else to know because I've seen what people do when someone they know has AIDS. They treat them differently, as though they're dying. I've got a lot more living to do yet, so I can do without all that negativity.'

I promised, but as the days went by, I couldn't get his death sentence out of my head, so I made an appointment with the grief counsellor.

'My son has a terminal illness,' I told her, loath to use the A-word, 'but my mind's already so full of grief there's just no room for any more. He doesn't want anyone else to know and that means I'm his only supporter. How can I cope?'

'I'm so sorry,' she responded. 'Your son has you to support him, but you need support as well. He should tell at least one other person, so you have someone else to share it with.'

Tony accepted the advice: 'Phil and Jenny have a brand-new baby, so I don't want to spoil this time for them, and Lynna and Doug's first baby's due in May. It will have to be Jane.'

So Jane it became, and her empathy and cheerful positivity would soften the deep sadness we shared as keepers of Tony's secret.

AIDS loomed as a one-way ticket to the grave with an array of barely understood tribulations to be borne along the way, so I tried not to look too far ahead. Tony kept the details of his illness to himself, as did many others, preferring to spare their families, perhaps fearing they'd be blamed for having brought it upon themselves. Keeping his status a secret thankfully also protected us from the discrimination and stigma that other families faced.

It was a poignant period in Tony's and my relationship. He'd been comfortable sharing his diagnosis with me, but he saw my attempts to mother him as smothering. His need for independence prevailed. He was the master weaver of his own life's tapestry, heightening the brighter hues, subduing the more sombre. Perhaps he believed that what he found challenging would for us be impossible. Perhaps he was right, and besides, he had another family he could turn to now, one who knew AIDS well: the strongly bonded gay community. They knew the obstacles, the challenges, the heartaches, and were always there, to share, to comfort and to support each other.

Endeavouring to maintain an 'all's well' façade, I got on with my life. I registered a name for my fast-expanding business, Blooming Gardens, worked long hours and took holidays to faraway places. I rode a grey horse high into the Andes, abseiled down a lava tube on a Galapagos island, and jostled through a market in Marrakech, distractions that not only helped heal my grief, but also provided much-needed respite from my fears for Tony's future.

Meanwhile, much became lost in the chasm. Tony kept to himself the fact that his lowered T-cell count had placed him in the category of people eligible for AZT (Retrovir), the only AIDS treatment available at the time. The drug had serious side effects, but it would keep him alive longer, hopefully until something better – possibly even a cure – came along. When he sometimes looked drawn and pale, I put it down to the toll the illness was taking on his fast-paced life, unaware he was taking AZT and that he was experiencing its taxing side effects. Those fortunate enough to be eligible for the rationed drug were provided with timers to remind them to take their four-hourly around-the-clock doses. If they were fortunate, they experienced only a couple of numerous possible reactions: anaemia, nausea, diarrhoea, dizziness, weakness, fatigue, muscle pain. Tony suffered diarrhoea so badly he often missed work, and nausea so severe that it affected his appetite and he lost weight. But there was no other option. He confided more in Jane than me, playing it down when he wrote to her. 'I'm okay thanks, Janie. The side effects of the medication I'm taking have diminished: just a slight anaemia, nothing to be alarmed about.'

Later in the year he returned to Bondi, elated to have successfully negotiated a new rental contract, this time with new flatmates Kevin and Vaughan on the upper level of an older-style block of four flats.

'You'll love my new flat,' he told me. 'The living room windows have views out over the beach. By the way, it's your birthday soon so you're invited for lunch, and I'll be doing the cooking.'

That lunch became a treasured memory. Tony tossed salad with a flourish as he joked with Kevin and Vaughan: 'These tuna steaks are cooked blue because they're at their most delicious that way.'

'Tony's a great flatmate,' Kevin told me. 'He's always bright and happy and when he tells me, "Life's out there to be lived, Kev", it cheers me up no end. If I'm tired when I get home he'll hand me a whisky and sit down to have one with me. He's good company.'

But the good times were not to last. One morning a few weeks later, it all unravelled. Tony had left his pills on the kitchen sink and Kevin discovered them.

'Tony, are you taking these pills? They're labelled AZT. I've heard about AZT – it's for treating AIDS. You don't have AIDS, do you?'

Tony couldn't lie. When he got up the following morning Kevin and Vaughan were waiting in the kitchen, grim-faced. 'We're sorry,

Tony, but we've decided we want you to leave. We all get along beautifully, but we just can't run the risk of having someone around here with AIDS. Please try to understand.'

So Tony was on the move again.

* * *

A bedsitter in inner-city Darlinghurst became Tony's new home, which he shared with his new flat-mate Caesar, a miniature schnauzer rescue dog, who accepted him, pills and all, with unquestioning devotion. Perhaps he was lonely initially, but soon his 'other' family began materialising around him, or perhaps he was converging with them at the very time they were galvanising into a united front.

He occasionally came to stay with me in Avalon, usually for a couple of days midweek, and never missed family get-togethers. He'd arrive by taxi with a bottle of champagne and entertain us better than any comedy routine, vying with Phil for the spotlight as they tried to outdo each other in outrageousness. While his siblings were absorbed in enjoying their quick-witted brothers, what I saw eluded them: the slimming of his frame, his slightly less rounded cheeks, the air of unspoken strain. I often wondered what lay beneath his veneer of cheerfulness, what toll AIDS was really taking.

1991

In the New Year, Keith phoned. 'Lesley, do you remember me having a large, dark mole on the right side of my neck?' he asked.

'No, not at all,' I replied.

'The doctor diagnosed it as a melanoma and removed it, but now he's discovered he didn't get it all, so I'm coming to Sydney for more surgery. He wants to know how long it's been there.'

I was certain I hadn't seen it during our marriage and suggested he ask Connie if she'd noticed it. I remembered those long Australian summers when everyone in our generation would lie in the sun for hours to get a suntan. We'd thought it was good for us.

One day as Keith lay recovering at Dee Why private hospital, there was a knock on his door. 'Come in,' he called.

The door swung open and in marched Tony, dressed in head waiter's garb, holding a large silver tray high on his right hand. Leaving it on the table in the corner of Keith's room, he returned a minute later with a wine stand, goblet and bottle of red wine.

'This is what you need, Dad. A good meal and a bottle of red can fix anything.' He proceeded to carve a rare beef fillet, which he served with vegies, horseradish, gravy and garnishes, fit for a gourmet, to a beaming, chuckling Keith. Tony loved his dad, and at last he'd found a way to express it.

* * *

Nothing could have prepared us for the tragic years that lay ahead. Everyone dreaded who'd be next, knowing AIDS lurked out there, like a python poised to strike, to silently squeeze out life. All who fell prey bore its stigma, as did their families and their loved ones. It was to St Vincent's Hospital they turned, seeking hope when none existed. The hospital was a stone's throw from Oxford Street, where Sydney's once vibrant gay community had lived and played for decades. Ward 17 South was the AIDS ward, and its team of dedicated doctors and nurses were ready to cope with every affliction the disease could deliver. AIDS took no prisoners. There was no cure. It was terminal.

Tony's move to Darlinghurst marked the beginning of significant change in his life. Now that he was in the heart of the gay community and at the epicentre of the AIDS crisis, his life as a warrior and activist was about to begin.

Part 3
The War

Tony Carden was my fellow activist in ACT UP. My own story as an AIDS activist in Sydney began when I was still living in Madison, Wisconsin. My first boyfriend, Geoffrey, whom I met when I was 21 in 1988, was HIV positive. Mine was the first generation of gay men who never knew a time before AIDS. You had a choice: join the growing grassroots movement against AIDS, or be a bystander, but even as a bystander, you still had AIDS in your face.

Yet I don't think I ever made a conscious choice to be an activist. I was swept up in a movement, one that saw lots of people surrender their normal lives because there was a war.

I met the bravest people I ever knew, people who risked jail or worse to get some little pill across borders or out of laboratories to the bodies of those too sick or too scared to hunt down their own treatment. Tony was one of those brave people, the most playful of any of us, with the best sense of humour.

I'm a professional composer. During the plague years, I had given up music in order to be an activist. But recently, I released a ninety-minute memoir of my AIDS activist years in the form of a string quartet. It contains reflections of historic events and portraits of activist friends now dead.

Tony's and my outspoken public personas were what people saw. But I wanted to remember his sensitive side, the way he cared for his dog Biche, his surprise gifts and cards to me to sustain our morale, and his extraordinary artwork *Warrior Blood*. My last memory directly related to him is playing the organ at his funeral, and that shows up in the soaring hymn-like chorale towards the end of the music I wrote for him.

Lyle Chan, from his *Warrior Blood* profile, 2014

ACT UP logo, 1991. Bright pink triangle and white lettering on black background.

Chapter 13

Light on the Shore

> Homophobia, deceit, racism, fear, jealousy – these few will do to begin with. When I became ill I realised for the first time that I had endured much of this throughout my life as if it were just part of my load to tug. Then presto change-o, I decided I will suffer no longer. I will act.
>
> Tony's journal, 1995

1990

The AIDS Council of New South Wales (ACON) was the lighthouse on the shore during Sydney's AIDS epidemic, shining out over unpredictable waters, a beacon for those living with HIV/AIDS. The keepers of the light included old hands Bill Whittaker and Don Baxter. Bill had moved on from being President of the Sydney Gay and Lesbian Mardi Gras to become ACON's first Executive Director, and Don brought to ACON many years of leadership experience within the gay community. Bill had seen ACT UP (AIDS Coalition to Unleash Power) in action when he'd visited New York City, where it had been founded in 1987. He'd seen its members come together as activists and witnessed how, despite their haphazard demonstrations, they'd wrested positive responses from a recalcitrant government and dollar-conscious drug companies.

Bill and Don were consummate organisers and diplomatic

people-handlers. They excelled in bringing to the table a range of players including immunologists, politicians, representatives of pharmaceutical companies, leaders of health organisations and community groups to negotiate constructive outcomes. But with the infection rate rising fast, and significant changes needed to stem it, Bill and Don recognised that there was a gap at the table, a vital missing link – those who were actually living and dying with the disease, those very people who in 1988 had pleaded, 'Talk TO us, not ABOUT us'.

Harbouring an ulterior motive, Bill organised a public meeting in the form of an AIDS information night. Anyone who turned up would learn about the dire urgency of the need for AIDS drugs and the challenge of making them available. Hopefully, as HIV positive people, they'd be sufficiently concerned for their own wellbeing to take up the gauntlet. Their input was now vital because they could agitate to keep politicians and policy makers on their toes in ways that ACON as a government-funded organisation could not.

One autumn evening, Tony joined a throng of over two hundred people heading to the basement carpark of ACON's Surry Hills office. By eight o'clock, the basement was full, with some people seated on plastic chairs, others huddled around pillars and along walls, chatting. The buzz hushed as Bill introduced Professor David Cooper, immunologist from St Vincent's Hospital, whose work had placed him at the frontline of the Australian AIDS epidemic.

Professor Cooper outlined the HIV/AIDS dilemma with brutal brevity. 'Under the present Australian drug evaluation program, it will be years before the medications you need to stay alive will become available.'

A silent shock of disbelief gripped the audience. Without medication they had no hope.

'I can't get the drugs you need unless the system changes and I can't change things by myself.'

Message delivered. Professor Cooper pleaded a hospital emergency and departed the meeting. The audience erupted into urgent conversation – what to do, how to get through to the government, and how to get the Pharmaceutical Benefits Scheme changed. Ross Duffin, long-time ACON volunteer, called the meeting to order and outlined the earlier achievements of ACT UP in New York. 'I move that we meet as soon as possible to form a Sydney chapter of ACT UP.'

Hands shot up like fireworks, all eager would-be seconders. Many had heard of ACT UP's successes in America so despite the sceptical view of a conservative few that its tactics were 'in your face', the motion was carried.

Two weeks later, around eighty people met in a room above the Arq Nightclub, a short distance from Oxford Street, usually a venue for musicians, drag-queen performers and cocktail-sipping concert-goers, but tonight it was anything but a night-club, with the audience focused only on starting a chapter of ACT UP in Sydney. Silence fell as Ross welcomed everyone and invited their input.

Tony rose to speak. An utter intolerance of unfairness in any shape or form had remained with him from his Pennryn days. As far as he was concerned, discriminatory treatment of society's vulnerable by those more powerful was totally unacceptable. For two decades it had been the raw nerve behind his jovial façade, and now, at 29, as he stood describing the people with AIDS he'd seen in New York, unable to afford drugs and lacking medical care, that nerve began to twitch. Unless they became pro-active, he warned them, they simply would not survive. 'If we don't help ourselves, we'll die' was his dramatic concluding pronouncement.

A former New Yorker Bruce Brown took the floor after Tony, describing first-hand his own experience of ACT UP in the US. Tony warmed immediately to Bruce, with his charisma and enthusiasm, and the two young men bonded that night in a friendship that would nurture ACT UP during the rocky years that lay ahead.

Enthusiastic applause greeted Amelia Menia, her appearance angelic beneath her fluff of strawberry-blonde hair. Amelia revealed herself to be someone they'd not expected that night: an HIV-positive woman. The gay community were keen to see heterosexuals join forces with them, to add a vital dimension to their common cause. The first heterosexual woman to 'come out' about her status, Amelia would also become Tony's close friend. Supported and empowered by ACT UP's energy, Amelia would later help found 'Positive Women', an organisation to give voice to women living with HIV/AIDS.

By the end of the meeting, agreement about the new ACT UP Sydney's mission was unanimous: to demand changes to the Australian drug-evaluation system so that drugs approved in America and stagnating in pharmaceutical companies' factories could be made available to people with HIV/AIDS in Australia.

It would be a huge challenge, they knew, but a cause they'd work towards with relish. Ross, a practical man and a journalist with press connections, added strength to the pool of talent surfacing that night, a core group that would enable ACT UP Sydney to take off. As in every group, there were a conservative few to counter any over-enthusiasm. They cautioned that too much banner-waving, fist-shaking and shouting might prove negative to their cause, but Tony had no intention of fist-shaking or shouting. He had more persuasive methods in mind.

As a group, they'd taken three huge strides: they'd inaugurated ACT UP Sydney; composed a tactfully worded letter congratulating the Minister for Community Services and Health, Brian Howe, on his appointment; and arranged their first protest: a 'die-in', to be staged outside the office of the federal health department. This was seen as a way to target, very publicly, the Australian Drug Evaluation Committee and to protest the lack of treatment access. Furthermore, they scheduled it to take place when the committee was in session, just two weeks hence.

Working as a waiter at Bilson's left Tony available during the daytime so putting aside a couple of auditions, he threw himself into preparing for the protest along with others no longer well enough to hold down full-time jobs. The group hurriedly pulled together the props they would need: coffins, banners and black ACT UP t-shirts emblazoned with a pink triangle above a white logo 'Silence = Death'. The downward-pointing pink triangle was chosen as a reminder of the symbol used by the Nazis to mark homosexuals out for persecution.

* * *

The day came and the twenty-eight eager activists were up early, each apprehensive about what lay ahead: excitement for some, anxiety for others. For Tony, the prospect of the protest was exhilarating, a perfect opportunity to exercise his performing skills; it would be unrehearsed, live theatre. He was off to perform! At 11 am one Friday in April 1990, with their banners discretely tucked away, they gathered outside 333 Kent Street, where the Australian Drug Evaluation Committee was in session.

By midday office workers were milling along the footpath when a truck arrived carrying seven coffins, which were calmly unloaded and evenly spaced across the building's front steps as though the Health Minister himself had ordered them. Between the coffins, along the steps, across the foyer and down the hallway, 'patients' took up their positions, then 'died' there on the floor as banners pronounced, 'People are dying of AIDS. We need Drugs NOW'.

Curious crowds congregated, the press arrived, police appeared. From the top step, Bruce arose from the dead to address the gathering, black megaphone in hand. 'Rationing life-saving drugs is un-Australian. We are dying because our drug-evaluation system is archaic. Drugs already approved in America should be made available to us NOW, not in two years' time because by then most of us will be dead. We've got nothing to lose, so for God's sake trial them on us, NOW.'

ACT UP Sydney's first protest screened on the TV news that night, and the next morning hit the newspapers. The public learned of their plight and heard their message loud and clear. The police had been tolerant, but Bruce had caught the flu, due, he believed, to having become chilled, lying on a cold concrete step. He later told Tony it was a small price to pay after such an empowering debut demonstration.

At the next ACT UP meeting the mood was celebratory; the battle to change Australia's drug-regulation system had now entered the public forum. Members agreed they'd made a powerful impression without falling foul of the law. Bill, aware of how pleased they felt with themselves, cautioned them: 'Focus on solving the drugs problem. It's the urgent one and it's vital. Don't let yourselves become distracted by other causes. They can keep.'

But the ever-constant bugbear of discrimination was difficult to condone. A month later a small group of activists protested outside Parramatta Gaol. How could they stand by and take no action against the compulsory HIV-testing of inmates while condoms, bleach and clean needles were unavailable within the prison? With help from the media, this issue also attracted public attention.

ACT UP protest against the delay in AIDS drugs approval, George Street, Sydney, 1990. Photo courtesy Jamie Dunbar

ACT UP Parramatta Gaol Protest, May 1991.
Photo courtesy Jamie Dunbar

Three days later the publicity around ACT UP's first demonstration produced some small fruit: federal Health Minister Brian Howe approached ACON to discuss AIDS drugs trials in Australia. ACT UP was off to a promising start.

In June, armed only with tubes of red lipstick to inscribe their message, ACT UP struck again, this time outside the US consulate to protest US government–imposed travel restrictions on people with HIV. This time the police, torn by their responsibility to protect the US consulate, were less tolerant. Seven arrests took place that day including of Bruce and Tony, who were beaten with batons and bundled into a paddy wagon with considerable loss of dignity. Despite this, they saw value in the experience. Although the protestors suffered from wounded pride and a few bruises, no charges were laid.

Members of The Wilderness Society, a co-tenant of the building where ACT UP members met weekly, were well honed in the arts of activism. The budding ACT UP activists gained valuable insights from those old hands into handling police intimidation and catching the media's attention without being arrested, skills they gratefully put to good use.

At subsequent meetings two new members introduced themselves: Claude Fabian, a costume-jewellery maker with substantial organisational skills, and composer Lyle Chan, who had arrived from the US already ACT UP-experienced. Lyle had put his music studies aside to undertake a course in molecular biology, which enabled him to contribute much-valued expertise on the topic of AIDS drugs. Lyle soon teamed up with Bruce and Tony to become ACT UP spokespeople, all three bringing experience from their previous careers: Tony would use his acting skills to make a theatrical event of every protest and demonstration; Bruce's performance flair would add charisma to his speeches, and Lyle's knowledge of AIDS medications would prove invaluable in tackling the drugs availability problem. Ross and Claude became the schemers, plotters and planners backed by a core group of thirty or so activists – it was a well-cast team of players.

If ever a group needed an angel in their midst it was Sydney's gay community during the AIDS crisis. Clover Moore had been elected to the New South Wales Legislative Assembly in 1988 as member for Bligh, an electorate encompassing the Eastern Suburbs of Sydney, including Darlinghurst. This meant Clover not only represented much of Sydney's gay community, but with ever-increased majorities, she'd be there for them for the duration of the AIDS epidemic. A skilled politician, Clover was a rare bird: credible, conscientious, caring, honest and, best of all, decent. She set up her electoral office not in seaside Bondi nor fashionable Edgecliff but in the heart of Darlinghurst, where her neediest constituents resided, and not far from St Vincent's Hospital.

Devastated by the anguish around AIDS, Clover made sure her door was always open to those who sought counsel. When Tony, as ACT UP's spokesperson, knocked on her door to deliver a copy of

ACT UP US Consulate Protest, Sydney, 1990.
Photo courtesy Jamie Dunbar

its mission statement, it was the beginning of a powerful friendship. Clover would soon become one of Tony's most trusted friends and allies.

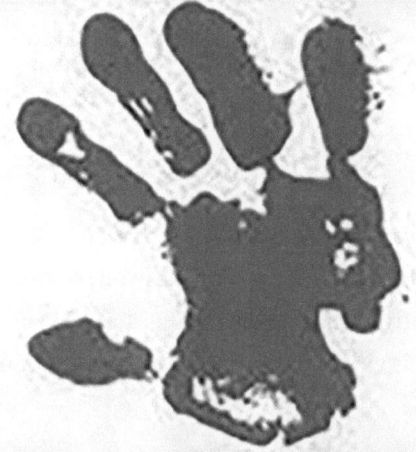

ACT UP New York poster, 1988.

Chapter 14

Buyers Club

> Years ago I watched friends die without any hope at all. Today this is no longer necessary. With early intervention of antiviral therapy, positive thinking and living, I can live with a realistic belief that this virus can be overcome. It's about taking responsibility from Day One.
>
> Tony's journal, 1995

1991

Living in Darlinghurst put Tony right at the heart of his new work. He could walk to ACT UP meetings, access 'Tiffany's Transport', the community bus to get to and from the AIDS Clinic at St Vincent's, and visit Clover's office whenever she needed a political nudge. He ate healthily and exercised daily, but the daily doses of AZT presented challenges: its side effects were so debilitating that sometimes he had no choice other than to give his body respite by not taking it for a month. Constant nausea and diarrhoea wore him down, and anaemia depleted his iron levels so that he twice needed a blood transfusion.

Some nights he was so unwell he'd call Bilsons to tell Judy he couldn't make it. While he'd stuck to his vow of secrecy, Judy had guessed he might be HIV-positive. She often begged him to 'be careful', and he always responded with a joke. She and Michael agreed that as long as he wished to continue to work with them, they'd provide the support he relied on to maintain his independence. Judy and Michael were loyal and supportive friends.

AIDS began to present other problems: thrush to plague Tony's gut and retinitis to blight his eyes. He stoically learnt to live with those but what he most dreaded was the spread of KS (Kaposi sarcoma), knowing that its malignant tentacles could creep not only into his arms, legs, face and throughout his body, but even to his brain.

I'd wondered why some people with AIDS developed KS and others didn't. It played on my mind unresolved until years later, when I realised that long-term survivors of the epidemic, including most of Tony's friends, hadn't succumbed to KS. Curious also about Tony's retinitis and remembering how ill he'd been with shingles earlier in the year, I'd investigated the herpes virus, only to stumble on a surprise fact: not only was herpes behind his retinitis but it was probably also the cause of his Kaposi sarcoma. I'd been aware of the forms of herpes that causes cold sores, thrush, chicken pox or, in older people, shingles, but I learnt that there are in fact eight-known herpes viruses, the latest recognised being human herpesvirus 8 (HHV-8), otherwise known as Kaposi sarcoma–associated herpesvirus (KSHV). It is sexually transmitted, and remains latent, sometimes for many years, until its carrier contracts the HIV virus, when it develops into Kaposi sarcoma.

I remembered with unease that when Tony's anxiety at Pennryn had begun, he'd also developed cold sores, for the first time in his life, symptoms of herpes.

* * *

ACT UP's protests around AZT had produced results, but they were grudgingly small: AZT was still rationed but had been made available to more patients. The downside was that in long-term users the drug was losing its potency and without something better, AIDS sufferers knew their chances were fading. What annoyed them most was that political stubbornness stood in their way. Dreading a repeat of the thalidomide tragedy of decades earlier, doctors and politicians were loath to approve new medications without a mandatory two-year testing period to exclude possible side effects. They were playing it safe. But as far as ACT UP was concerned, they were playing it too safe. Those who needed AIDS drugs were terminally ill anyway. They needed them now and were willing to become guinea-pigs to trial the drugs because they had nothing to lose.

So gaining access to two new antiviral drugs ddI (didanosine) and ddC (dideoxycytidine) became ACT UP's next goal. They were prepared to be as brazen as they needed to be to make these life-savers available, and why stop at just these? Other medications quickly joined their list: anti-fungal drugs to fight thrush; drugs to keep the usually fatal AIDS-related PCP pneumonia at bay and others.

'It's crazy,' complained Tony. 'More and more of us are dying every week, while drugs that have already been trialled and approved in the US and could save our lives are being withheld because of bureaucracy. It's sheer bloody-mindedness!'

Just as they were contemplating the possibility of another demonstration, an ideal opportunity presented itself: the Fourth National AIDS Conference, to be held in Canberra.

'It's perfect,' concluded Bruce. 'When we link up with Canberra's and Melbourne's ACT UP chapters, we'll become a force to be reckoned with.'

In August several carloads of Sydney ACT UP-ers drove to Canberra, where they joined activists from Melbourne and Canberra as ACT UP Australia, bristling to present their demands at the Fourth National Conference on AIDS.

When federal Health Minister Brian Howe stood to deliver his televised speech, four hundred people walked silently onto the stage, each laying a red rose at the minister's feet, while banners demanded 'FAST-TRACK HIV/AIDS MEDICATIONS NOW TO SAVE LIVES'. All was going well until, overcome by anger, several militant protestors upended some of the pharmaceutical companies' stands, releasing an avalanche of pill boxes and pamphlets. The mood became nasty, and the press was there to capture it on film as the debacle cast ACT UP in a dismal light. Recognising the need for some face-saving action, Bruce quickly took the stage and pleaded for compassion. He redeemed the day. The audience empathised, and Bruce received a standing ovation.

It was another successful protest, and despite the close shave, another step towards breaking down the minister's resistance to change. Tony was elated.

A few weeks later ACT UP members reinforced the message in Pitt Street Mall in the Sydney business district. With banners held high, they again demanded action over the lack of access to ddI and ddC. Police stood by as a lunchtime crowd collected, reporters waited with pens and notebooks poised and cameras pointed.

Tony, clad in pyjamas and dressing-gown, raised his megaphone. 'Withholding these drugs is killing people. That's a crime against humanity and the Australian Government is the party guilty of that crime.'

As they did before every protest, ACT UP had issued a press release the previous afternoon to ensure that the police and press, now considered allies, would arrive to guarantee maximum coverage for their ruse. That evening the Australian public received a visual update on TV newscasts about the inhumane situation. Public opinion was being inflamed, and politicians were becoming edgy.

1990/1991

During the Christmas/New Year holiday period, media focus on the AIDS crisis had waned so Lyle, Tony, new member Kirsty Machon and several others decided to boost ACT UP's publicity. With minimal disruption and a degree of confident aplomb, they took over the Department of Health's switchboard in early February. Lyle presented flowers to surprised switchboard operators as the activists read a prepared statement to callers in a demonstration less militant but just as successful as their feistier protests in eliciting empathy from the public.

* * *

Buoyed by fresh publicity about the success of their year-long battle to break the AIDS drugs drought, members at ACT UP's first meeting for the year were bristling for a fresh challenge.

'Maybe it's time we tackled the Anti-Discrimination Board,' suggested Bruce. 'So far they've dodged every case of discrimination against AIDS sufferers and homosexual people that's come their way, so let's put them on notice.'

A round of applause was followed by two hours of animated discussion as a new demonstration evolved.

Tony described it to me years later: 'Early in 1991 ACT UP began by displaying posters calling for volunteers to "STORM THE ADB". Thirty-two activists responded. We all wore surgical masks and yellow rubber gloves, and we marched into the ADB's headquarters – an old brick building in Sydney's CBD – and headed straight up the stairs and into the office of the Board's President. He was sitting at his desk shuffling papers, and as we closed the door, he jumped up. You should have seen the look on his face! He looked panic-stricken.' Tony chuckled, remembering. 'We said nothing, just stood in a row in front of him until he sat down again. By then I reckon he was turning rather pale. Eventually one of us stepped forward, put out her hand and presented him with a large manila envelope. He opened the envelope and took out the two official-looking notices that were inside. The first one condemned the board's lack of action on HIV-related discrimination, and the second advised them that ACT UP would be closely monitoring the progress of the public enquiry he'd promised and the legislative changes that were supposed to take place. And that wasn't the end of it because after a few weeks of no action, ACT UP slapped a large notice of eviction across the building's entrance.'

Years later, researching ACT UP's archives, I came across a copy of that notice:

> **NOTICE OF EVICTION TO THE NSW ANTI-DISCRIMINATION BOARD**
> Notice is hereby given that on Thursday 14th February 1991 at 1.30 pm the ADB is to immediately vacate these premises.
>
> The Board has been abolished because it has failed to take any action to stop HIV/AIDS-related discrimination:
> - The Board has never held an enquiry into this matter.
> - After ten years of the AIDS epidemic the Board has done nothing to push for legislation outlawing HIV/AIDS-related discrimination.
>
> AIDS COALITION TO UNLEASH POWER (ACT UP)
>
> WE ARE NOT SILENT

* * *

Tony's need for a second drug was becoming life-or-death urgent. AZT's side effects were wearing him down. He looked twice at the headlines in the July edition of the *Sydney Star Observer*: 'ACON Announces Scheme to Assist Importing AIDS Drugs.' What breakthrough had they discovered, he wondered. It was in fact a short clause buried in a voluminous NSW Government drugs availability review. Changes in legislation meant it was now possible to import supplies of a drug from overseas, under strict conditions. ACON had spotted this passage and had jumped on it.

An information letter was sent to the seasick sailors on ACON's list of people struggling with HIV/AIDS:

'The attached information relates to changes in the *Therapeutic Goods Act*, which came into force in February of this year. It is now possible for individuals to import three months' supply of a drug at their own expense, provided they have an Australian script from a doctor in their state of residence.'

Attached was an application form for financial assistance and a release form to protect ACON from being seen as suppliers.

Tony eagerly grasped this lifeline of hope. He took leave from work, obtained scripts with repeats for six months' supply of ddC, withdrew a chunk of his savings and bought a ticket to New York via San Francisco. He tossed minimal clothing into his blue suitcase, along with a pile of other peoples' scripts and, with plenty of room in his near-empty bag for the medications he planned to carry on his return journey, jumped into my car for a ride to the airport, supposedly for a holiday to visit his New York friends. As he disappeared into airport's men's room he winked at me, declaring, 'Just wait, Lezzles. I'll be upgraded to first class. You'll see.'

He reappeared a suave businessman in a dark suit, blue business shirt and tie, no hint of drug-smuggler about him. He was duly upgraded.

Once in the US, he visited Lyle's contacts to get scripts filled, caught up with his New York City friends and saw as many Broadway shows as he could fit in. He knew there was a chance his life-saving load would be confiscated by customs officers, even though they had no right to question how he'd obtained them, but he also knew he was entitled to carry his goods as long as the name and address on every package matched that on an accompanying doctor's prescription. Fortunately, he breezed through the customs inspection and took his heavy suitcase of drugs directly to ACON for quality testing. Thanks to the suit and Tony's aplomb in portraying himself as a smooth businessman, the trip had been a success.

Under Lyle's expertise, with Ross Duffin managing the scripts, and adventurous volunteers like Tony, Sydney's 'buyers club' took off, so named after the famous 'Dallas Buyers Club' started by American Ron Woodroof, who'd contracted HIV in 1985. With his health in fast decline, Ron had found his way onto a clinical trial of AZT when it first became available in the US. He suffered such debilitating side effects that he dropped out of the trial, labelling the drug 'toxic'. But Woodroof was not to be beaten. He ferreted out whatever other drugs and herbal remedies he could lay his hands on, and devised his 'Dallas Buyers Club,' whereby HIV-positive people could join, pay a monthly fee and in return receive drugs to fight their illness. His efforts brought stays of execution for many. Woodroof travelled the globe, keeping just one step ahead of the law, to obtain and deliver otherwise unavailable medications to a grateful HIV-positive community.

Within weeks, hundreds were submitting their scripts to ACON, and legal 'smugglers' like Tony were crossing the Pacific as lifesavers.

* * *

Respite was golden, and singing offered solace and provided a good way to let off steam, so from among Darlinghurst's community arose the Gay and Lesbian Choir, which was to make its debut singing for the 'Blessing of Mardi Gras', as a counterbalance to Fred Nile's prayers for rain. Throughout the years of the epidemic the choir's membership swelled until it was singing worldwide, its moving chorales establishing it as a world-famous choir. Their music soared, drowning out the despair of AIDS.

No Gays Please, We're Tasmanian

HOBART: Homosexual sex is to remain a criminal offence in Tasmania, with a minimum penalty of 21 years' jail.

Defying the national trend, the state's Upper House last night rejected the HIV/AIDS Preventive Measures Bill, which would decriminalise such acts.

Tasmania is now the only state to retain such an offence, described in its Criminal code as 'carnal knowledge of any person against the order of nature'.

The decision comes three years after a heated debate began in Tasmania, and nine years after NSW decriminalised homosexual sex. Victoria dropped the offence eleven years ago.

The Sydney Morning Herald, 4 July 1991

Chapter 15

No Room at the Inn

> I work seven day a week in AIDS activism. It's important for me and I believe that when I'm doing something positive I'm doing something good for my health as well.
>
> But of course I couldn't do any of it without my carers Andrew and Tracey. They're fantastic. A lot of the credit for what I manage to do should definitely go to them.
>
> Tony, speaking to AñA Wojak, 1991

1991

Initially ddC brought Tony a resurgence of energy, boosting his morale enough for him to push AIDS into the background for a while, despite knowing that in time the virus's Jekyll-and-Hyde mutability would eventually send him in pursuit of yet another drug, probably ddI. Then after that, what? Researchers and pharmaceutical companies were plodding on together looking for new drugs and rediscovering new uses for old ones. Occasionally they hovered around a potential answer, but so far they'd been unable to come up with a cure. Now, as the epidemic gathered momentum, Tony and others in the same predicament were hanging on, hoping the parts of the puzzle would fit together before their time ran out.

Eventually Tony's health became too compromised for him to continue to work. Reluctantly, he knew the time had come to bid

Bilson's farewell. Judy, Michael and Tony Bilson, the owner/manager of Bilson's threw a party to wish him well, and as champagne corks popped, he pushed to the back of his mind the realisation that this loss in income might cost him much of his freedom.

Despite concerns about money and health, Tony maintained his superficial joviality and his 'all's-well' façade until one night he woke in the early morning hours with a pounding heart, barely able to breathe. He called a taxi, used an ACON cab voucher to get to St Vincent's Hospital and stumbled into the emergency department. He was classified triage one, but when he told the nurse of his AIDS status, he was hastily placed on a trolley and wheeled to a small, isolated alcove, where he remained untended until I arrived two hours later. I asked the nurse why he'd been treated this way.

'There are no vacant beds for patients with your son's condition, so he'll just have to stay there,' she told me. 'His heart has settled down, so we think what he's experiencing is a panic attack.'

Tony was angry. He'd watched several other patients receive treatment and be allocated beds in appropriate wards; it seemed it was only HIV/AIDS patients who couldn't be catered for. He phoned Bruce for some support, and the three of us returned to his apartment to sit out the night while Tony recovered.

The following day he came home with me. I could see as we lunched on the deck that something was on his mind so I asked him about it. He looked grim:

'Things won't be easy for me now I'm not working any more. I'm sure I'd be eligible for an invalid pension, but after I pay $40 a week for AZT and more every three months for ddC, there won't be much left. If you, Phil and Keith could contribute enough to make another $100, I'd be okay. How would you feel about that?'

'Leave it with me, Tony. I'll set things up with Phil and Keith. Oh, and I'll pay your electricity and phone bills, too. That should make things easier.'

Whether a product of living only in the present because the future might never happen, whatever money Tony had in his pocket always evaporated within hours, so I kept my cash handouts to small amounts and instead took care of his Oxford Street pharmacy account. The list of bills grew longer by the month as Tony discovered extra tempting items. When receipts for Ella Baché cosmetics began appearing I suspected him of 'dressing up'. A memorable snippet from his notebook I later discovered showed his attitude to shopping:

'Don't deny yourself anything, and if you think it's too small it probably is.'

But the sad reality was that he was trying to hide the unsightly lesions of Kaposi sarcoma. It worked well because I never again noticed any purple blotches. It was likewise with an expensive teeth-whitening gel, but when he explained how badly AZT was staining his teeth, I contributed enthusiastically towards maintaining the sparkle of his smile.

He later approached Ella Baché, complimenting the company on how successfully their product could be used to conceal KS's purple blotches, whereupon they agreed to make their out-of-date products available at a token price to grateful AIDS patients.

To coincide with his return from St Vincent's AIDS Clinic via the community bus, I'd wait outside his flat with a box of food and a bone for Caesar and invite him to stroll with me up to Oxford Street for lunch. Urbane Oxford Street was as foreign to me then as an Istanbul market and I felt like a trespasser, walking along the crowded footpaths among jaunty, self-possessed gay guys, past 'leather' shops and upstairs S&M venues. All were mysteries to me then: the feathers and suspender-belts, wigs and whips, leather and chains.

One afternoon I arrived at his flat to find a fire truck parked in the laneway outside, a thick hose propping the door open. I rushed in through curling grey smoke and saw with relief the charred remains of a small fire on the carpet at the end of Tony's bed. A fireman was tending to Tony's burnt arm as Caesar looked on, tail wagging.

'Whatever's happened? Is he okay?'

'Thankfully we got here in time. Are you his mother?'

Tony sat on an ottoman in the darkened room looking dazed, his blistering, red arm resting on a cushion. From his mutterings, the blackened carpet and small twisted radiator I pieced together what had happened: He'd been prescribed the narcotic painkiller pethidine to self-inject when the pain in his eyes from retinitis became unbearable. He'd injected the drug and laid on the bed to wait for the pain to subside, then Caesar had barked, alarming him. He'd seen the radiator, glowing red, so had got up to turn it off and in his narcotic daze had stumbled. The radiator had overturned and ignited the carpet with Tony sprawled on top.

'I think I remember calling triple-0,' he said vaguely. 'Or maybe it was a neighbour because of the smoke. There was a hell of a lot of it.'

On the way to St Vincent's, I asked whether he was okay because he was looking down, shielding his face. He squinted at me through half-closed eyes and asked, 'Would you mind lending me your sunglasses? Retinitis is pretty painful and it makes my eyes extremely light-sensitive.'

On our arrival he advised the triage nurse of his AIDS status and was once again wheeled to the far corner of the emergency department to wait several hours more before a nervous intern arrived to dress his burns.

This incident must have dashed his confidence, because it spurred him into taking steps to make his life easier. He visited Clover and put his name on the public housing list.

Home for the next three years became an old sandstone building in Woolloomooloo that was once a corner shop, converted into a small two-level house with a tiny garden and an out-house toilet, now a garden shed. Carved into the sandstone above the corner door was a reminder of its original owner: George Barker, 1887.

Fronting a swathe of village-green grass and trees, and surrounded by terrace houses, Tony's new home was within walking distance of Oxford Street and St Vincent's and, best of all, in proximity to two local pubs. The Frisco Hotel, once a watering hole for American merchant

Tony's Housing Commission home, Woolloomooloo. 1991.
Graffiti and broken windows were common practice in Woolloomooloo
during the era of AIDS-related homophobia.

seamen, boasted an iron lace–fronted verandah where we'd sometimes sit on sunny days for lunch; and The Tilbury, home of bawdy cabarets, was where we'd spend occasional light-hearted evenings singing along over dinner. When we attended the Opera House, we'd saunter home through the spookily dark Botanic Gardens and down the steep Fleet Steps to Woolloomooloo.

Tony's next port of call was the office of Community Support Network (CSN) to request some volunteer assistance so that he wouldn't have to exhaust his waning energy reserves on cleaning, shopping and cooking. He needed to preserve what strength he had for ACT UP.

Thus entered into Tony's life – following his rejection of three applicants as 'too pedestrian' – the pragmatic, capable and caring Andrew Bredin, and his co-volunteer, Qantas stewardess Tracey.

'Our attitude with clients was normally "take what you're given",' recalled Andrew, 'but Tony treated our interview as though he was hiring staff. When I began caring for him it was easy to see that his energy was easily spent, but he used his acting ability to mask his complaints. He appreciated our help but also required rapport and good company and, like most people with AIDS, he preferred his peers to look after him so that his family would be spared his suffering. He didn't allow his dogs, first Caesar and later Biche, to go out in case they picked up some bug like the cytomegalovirus from the footpaths, so I used to wrap their feet in nylon stockings to take them for a walk.'

Oxford Street was such an exotic place that a stern-faced charcoal-grey schnauzer or a fluffy white Bichon Frisé wearing nylon stockings barely merited a second glance.

Andrew's four-day CSN training had taught him how to turn a patient, give a bed bath and maintain AIDS-level standards of home hygiene, including pouring boiling water over washed dishes on the sink's drainage board. Cutlery was placed in a cup or glass, handles down, and also given the boiling-water treatment to protect frail immune systems from infection. I learnt to do likewise and still do, if only to remind myself of Tony and those dicey days.

Andrew Bredin, CSN Volunteer Carer, Woolloomooloo, 1994.

Anti-gay crime wave sweeps Sydney

Sydney's gay heartland is in the grip of an unprecedented wave of violent murders and bashings. Teenage gangs, straight from the nightmare world of *A Clockwork Orange*, are terrorizing the yuppie eastern and inner-city suburbs. Police, residents and gay groups are mobilizing against further mayhem.

The stories are always the same. The king hit, the thudding boots, and then the blood-stained pavements. Sometimes it's the hospital, sometimes the morgue.

KILLED – William Allen, 50, outside a toilet block in Alexandria Park.

KILLED – Krisha Korn, a 34-year-old Thai kitchenhand, punched and kicked at South Head before meeting his death at the bottom.

KILLED – John Russell, 31, whose body was found at the base of South Bondi cliffs.

The Sydney Morning Herald, 14 April 1991

Chapter 16

'Take No Bullshit'

As Australians we are known throughout the world for giving everyone a fair go, a chance. Our country enjoys one of the most diverse cultures in the world but if this diversity is to continue and flourish there is no room for discrimination on any level, towards any culture or any minority. We must all fight to extinguish it.

Tony's speech at launch of
Anti-Discrimination Campaign, 1993

June 1991

Desperation drove ACT UP to it because the demand they'd put to Brian Howe, federal Minister for Health, to break the drug-supply deadlock still hadn't been met. In each capital city ACT UP posters began appearing in newspapers, on power poles, as hand-outs and in windows of shops and businesses:

> **D Stands for Deaths Drugs Delays Deadline**
> A letter for Mr Howe, federal Minister for Health – ACT UP has a letter for Mr Howe. The letter is D. The letter stands for lots of things. Like Deadline. And D-Day. And Date – Thursday, 6th June 1991. By that date he will have delivered on our demands. Our demands are few. We just want drugs

for life-threatening conditions to be made available without Delay. The current situation is a Disaster.

Look for the D.

D-Day, 6 June 1944, when the Allied armies had landed in France, was the turning point in a united struggle against tyranny, so ACT UP chose its anniversary as the perfect date for their own D-Day. ACT UP branches nationwide liaised with each other in every state except Queensland, which had no branch. Queensland's Premier, Joh Bjelke-Peterson, had banned demonstrations and also declared, 'There are no homosexuals in Queensland. I am against the dirty and despicable acts these homosexual people carry out. You can't get any beast or animal that is so depraved as to carry on the way they do'.

Queensland's gay men either retreated deeply into their closets and slammed the doors or fled to New South Wales.

As dawn's first glow silvered Melbourne's skyline on 6 June, early-morning joggers came to a halt when they reached their much-loved Floral Clock in the Queen Victoria Gardens: yesterday's marigolds and petunias had disappeared and overnight had bloomed in their stead a garden full of small white crosses. Within two hours the press had joined a gathering crowd of curious office workers, and the hosts of Melbourne's breakfast news were announcing D-Day's first strike.

During the early hours of that same morning, Tony, Bruce, Ross and several other well-prepared activists had driven to Canberra for what would become the news of the day: a protest at Parliament House.

The Australian flag flapped in the cold breeze above Parliament House's rolling green lawns. In the House of Representatives, Prime Minister Bob Hawke was extolling the year's achievements of his Minister for Health Brian Howe, unaware that in doing so he'd pulled the trigger the thirty-three activists occupying the front rows of the public gallery had been waiting for.

They blew whistles and released red streamers to spiral out over MPs' heads, to cries of: 'AIDS drugs now', 'You've got blood on your hands' and 'You're a murderer, Mr Howe'. Two athletic volunteers, putting into practice a stunt they'd been working on for days, leapt over the gallery's railing and landed precariously but upright on the chamber's floor. They silently proceeded to hand out leaflets proclaiming their life-or-death demands. MPs, some irate, others terrified, cringed at the possibility that AIDS might erupt among them, as attendants hastily wriggled their hands into yellow rubber gloves.

'The civil disobedience will continue until we get a direct response from Canberra and the drug-approval system is freed,' the activists declared. Prime Minister Hawke, despite glaring at his Minister for Health, was surprisingly tolerant. In the press gallery, a throng of reporters milled around Tony and Bruce.

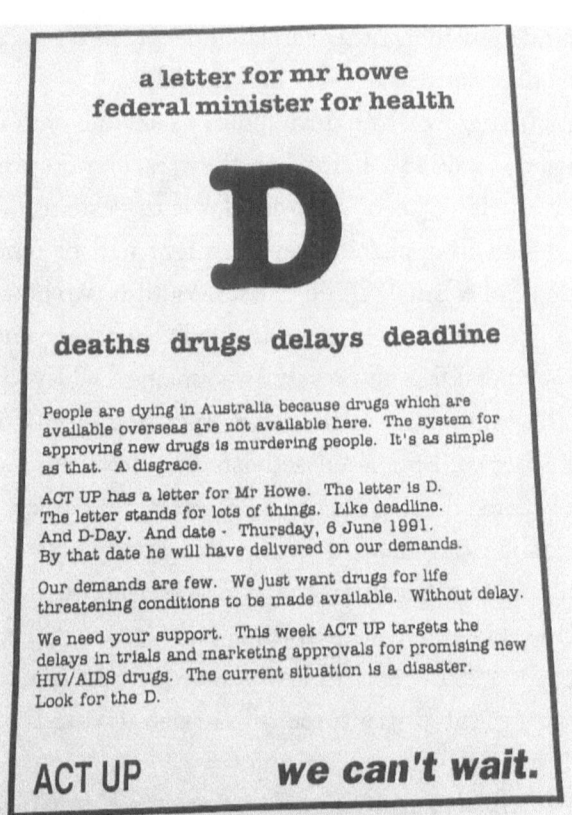

ACT UP D-Day poster, 1991.

'Of the eighty AIDS treatment drugs commonly in use overseas, only eight are available here,' Tony told them. 'The government should allow medications to be used in Australia as soon as they're approved by a competent overseas testing body.'

'ACT UP wants the government to stop insisting on a separate testing process in Australia. The Pharmaceuticals Act must be changed to allow people to stay alive,' added Bruce.

The following morning the message the press had been given was reported Australia-wide. Every ACT UP D-Day protest was covered: the Parliament House Protest; the Floral Clock replanting; a Martin Place 'die-in' organised by Lyle; and a demonstration in Perth led by thirty-three 'Sisters of Perpetual Indulgence'[17] – gay men, some bearded, dressed as nuns in black veils and nun's habits – who waved D-Day placards outside Minister Howe's Perth office.

The following month the government capitulated: they announced they would adopt reforms to expedite the process of making drugs available to AIDS patients.

The battle had been hard-won but ACT UP had achieved its goal.

* * *

Three weeks later, the meeting room of the Surry Hills Community Hall was abuzz. ACT UP members were presenting D-Day debriefing reports so exuberantly that the stranger sitting quietly in their midst went unnoticed, until a coffee break, when AñA Wojak raised a hand and asked permission to speak.

AñA was an artist on a mission to find a suitable model for a portrait of Saint Acacius, next in the series of portraits of Catholic saints for the art exhibition 'Stigmata'. AñA saw similarities between ACT UP's battles and the crusade of the fourth-century Acacius – both were

---

17 The Sisters of Perpetual Indulgence is a charity, protest and street performance organisation.

fighting for the rights of others: ACT UP for the survival of people living with AIDS, and Acacius to save the lives of his Christian followers facing execution for their beliefs. AñA had a hunch that an ACT UP meeting might be a good place to find a model.

No stranger to AIDS, AñA had already lost several friends to the illness and was deeply aware of the pain they'd suffered and the hopelessness that had accompanied their journeys.

AñA's hunches as to where to find subjects with qualities similar to those the particular historical or mythical saint was reputed to have possessed had so far proved right: in a dingy Kings Cross alley AñA had discovered a transsexual street worker, stoically accepting her fate, who'd accepted an invitation to sit for a portrait of the Virgin Mary; several months later AñA had met amongst some homeless people a feisty Maori girl who had agreed to pose as the courageous Saint Joan of Arc.

Tony felt an immediate rapport with Saint Acacius – a gutsy man of the cloth who'd done a deal with God to restore his followers to health and vitality – just as ACT UP was battling with the authorities for medications for the health and vitality of AIDS sufferers. To portray the exotic Acacius was a role Tony could not resist, so at the end of the meeting, he offered to sit for AñA's portrait.

Years later AñA explained, 'It was always bit risky because I didn't want the wrong person, but usually the right person stepped up.'

Over the next few weeks, AñA left the tranquillity of a waterfront cottage in bushland Maianbar, on the southern outskirts of Sydney, to visit Darlinghurst, so that artist and subject could get to know each other better.

'We hung out together so I could get his essence. We went to cafes and bars, and I got to experience firsthand what AIDS discrimination was all about. It surprised me because it was something that hadn't surfaced in Maianbar.'

During the first modelling session, Tony stood for a long period attired in a flowing, long-sleeved white gown, with only an occasional limber break. AñA had posed him carefully, standing tall with head erect and hands outfaced to reveal the halo and stigmata that would later be added. Working from various angles, AñA took photographs and made sketches of Tony to capture the fine details of his face, hands, eyes and posture.

From a trove of old cedar doors and tables painstakingly reclaimed over time from old houses, both inner-city and rural, and stored under the house, AñA chose the 'canvas', a weathered cedar table. Following traditional pre-Renaissance painting techniques, AñA applied the first of many layers of gold leaf, followed by a blue oil paint derived from lapis lazuli. Both would be used to achieve the glowing effect that was sought, working up from the bare surface of the table and allowing each layer to dry completely before adding the next. To perfect, each layer required hours of rubbing and blending, a procedure that caused strain, and often pain, to AñA's hands, lengthening the process further. *Acacius (Stigmata) – Portrait of Tony Carden* remained on AñA's easel for many weeks before it was ready for entry into the exhibition.

* * *

The activists had worked tirelessly – now it was time for them to play. Few communities could better balance their trials and traumas with such gay abandon as Oxford Street's, recalled Tony's carer Andrew Bredin years later as we chatted in his shady courtyard garden.

Barely a Saturday night went by during the '80s and '90s without a dance party where people could let off steam and put HIV/AIDS aside for a while. Organisers with such evocative labels as 'Paradise Garage', 'RAT Parties', 'Black Parties' and 'Bacchanalia' offered respite to those weighed down by the daily burden of living with HIV and to others living in dread of it. They would hire a venue, arrange a band or a DJ and install decorations: balloons, streamers, strobe lighting, smoke-machines, occasionally a huge chandelier – anything to create an atmosphere of exotica. Ads would appear in shop windows, bars, pubs, even on power poles to ensure the most essential ingredient: a crowd of patrons. Hundreds of guests would arrive at larger venues like the Hordern Pavilion or the Showground's Exhibition Hall to 'dance 'til you drop', often until dawn. Boot-Skootin' was the most popular dance style because it encouraged informality and improvisation.

Tony preferred smaller, invitation-only parties held in warehouses, where he often presented completely leather-clad, from his shiny black peaked cap, high-collared buttoned jacket and tight pants down to his knee-high black boots.

Some nights when the mood took him, his alter ego Crystal Loy, the illegitimate daughter of Hollywood's Myrna Loy, would appear instead, ash-blonde hair swept into a voluminous chignon and held in place with a bejewelled comb, and wearing a white satin shift, pearl necklace, dangling sparkly earrings and high-heeled silver

Tony as Crystal Loy

sandals – a voluptuous creature, usually on the arm of a proud partner for a night out on the town. Occasionally, when Tony was miffed by politics, Nirvana Trust would appear, with short, brown bobbed hair and minimal make-up, wearing a pink twinset and pleated skirt, and answering only to 'Miss Trust'. Whenever Nirvana arrived at a meeting, it was a reminder that something dubious was in the wind and needed looking into.

Crystal became so much a part of Tony's life that he named his Woolloomooloo house 'the Crystal House', nailing a gold-lettered plaque to the back wall and attaching a high-heeled sparkly sandal beneath. When I'd visit him, I'd smile at the shoe, naïvely unaware of his alter egos, which would only be revealed to me years later.

* * *

For the gay community, homophobic discrimination was the worst 'D' of all. They lived in its shadow, denying who they were, living secret lives, with some choosing suicide over social rejection. HIV/AIDS paranoia had heightened their torment, seeing them denied basic rights in areas such as housing and employment. Clover Moore, ever mindful of the wellbeing of her constituents, empathised with their harassment and decided she'd take a stand, knowing that a political battle lay ahead. Her determination was boosted by ACT UP's assurance that they and the gay community would back her every inch of the way. Gloves on!

At the time rumours were rife that a number of off-duty policemen, under cover of darkness, batons in hand, had joined groups of 'poofter bashers' as they patrolled 'gay beats' in parks and back streets to flog, sometimes kill, innocent victims. Investigations into the deaths of several gay men, during which witnesses were not interviewed and evidence quietly disappeared, arrived at verdicts of suicide. Teenage 'poofter bashers', following the examples of their elders, were similarly of the opinion that there was 'nothing wrong with it'. Homophobia rampaged unchallenged.

One night Tony was enjoying a quiet drink with friends at an Oxford Street hotel bar. A couple of cross-dressers sat on stools nearby, but the barman wasn't having a bar of their attire.

'Look at you, you pair of poofters. Types like you aren't welcome here. Get out of here before you're thrown out.'

Tony went to their rescue to defend their rights. The doorman grabbed him, hustled him through the door, threw him onto the footpath and began to bash him.

'You'd better stop right now, mate,' threatened Tony, 'because I've got AIDS and if you make me bleed I'll make sure you get it too.'

The thug stopped his hairy fist mid-swing, leaving Tony on the footpath bruised but with no blood spilt. Quick thinking had saved him. He'd been lucky where many others had not. With 'poofter bashers' roaming Darlinghurst's streets by night and police seldom responding to back-alley calls for help, most gay men and women had become loath to be out and about after dark.

Michael Glynn, *Sydney Star Observer*'s pragmatic founder and editor, realised that the gay community needed to take action. He called a meeting to address the issue of Darlinghurst's unsafe streets. Michael laid it on the line: 'Individually we're at risk but united we can protect ourselves.'

Following Michael's suggestion attendees agreed to form a community-based volunteer 'street patrol'. Each volunteer took a donated whistle from a box, and dozens, including Tony, joined the roster. They'd taken a stand against the Big D. Clover was planning to do likewise, in her own way.

* * *

If Clover Moore was the gay community's angel, the Reverend Fred Nile, leader of the Christian Democratic Party, was the devil in disguise. Fred's deep-seated intolerance of homosexuality and leading of public demonstrations against the gay community sparked Tony's ire.

Fred focused his attention on Sydney's Gay and Lesbian Mardi Gras, which he saw as a blatant display of wickedness. When his attempts to ban it failed, he resorted to annual 'prayers for rain' to dampen the parade or, even better, to wash it away completely. Fred was to Sydney what Joh Bjelke-Petersen was to Queensland, but unlike Joh, Fred had met with stiff opposition. In July he tried yet again to thwart the Mardi Gras by putting a motion to the New South Wales Parliament to have it banned. Again, he failed.

Not to be beaten, he rallied a 1,000-strong crowd of Christians of various denominations to meet in Hyde Park and march along the route of the Mardi Gras to Oxford Street, proclaiming through megaphones: 'Have mercy on our nation', 'Cleanse the city', 'They know not what they do', 'Fred knows what God hates', 'Adam and Eve, not Adam and Steve'.

When Fred and his cohort reached Oxford Street they were confronted by mounted police and a far larger army, including Tony, outnumbering Fred's by five to one and proclaiming: 'Gay love is best, go to hell Fred', 'Tolerance and Acceptance', 'Fred go away. I was born gay', 'We are gay, we are proud', 'Spank me. I'm Gay', 'Love rules the world'.

As the conflict heated up, eggs were thrown, Fred's microphone was grabbed by an activist and in the midst of the maelstrom the Sisters of Perpetual Indulgence calmly swept the street with brooms to 'clear away the homophobia'.

At the 1989 Mardi Gras a large papier-mache model of Fred's head had appeared, borne high on a silver salver. I remembered Tony's childhood papier-mache skills and wondered if he had been involved.

* * *

If Tony's slimming body, protruding cheekbones and pale complexion had caught the eye of any of our family, they kept their suspicions to themselves. For almost two years Jane and I had honoured our promise to keep his secret. Then one day Tony unwittingly blew his own cover.

In December 1991, Jenny and Phil threw him a thirtieth birthday party. Itty, a friend since *Bye Bye Birdie* days, was sitting beside Tony, her six-month-old son Max playing on her knee. The party was in full swing; there was plenty of food, the champagne was flowing, laughter filled the air, a happy air of joie de vivre permeated the room. Itty picked up Tony's glass of mineral water to offer a sip to baby Max, and in a panic Tony grabbed the glass, splashing water across the table as he yelled, 'No, Itty! He mustn't drink out of my glass.'

The laughter and chatter came to a sudden stop as all eyes converged on Tony. He had inadvertently announced what had remained unspoken for two years. Gradually the festivities resumed, but Tony's mute cat had escaped its bag.

Jane, Phil and Lynna suggested we keep the news from Mary, my mother and Tony's grandmother, now over eighty and widowed, to spare her the grief it would surely bring. But I argued that she should be told. The next time we met I broke the news as gently as I could. Mary had heard of AIDS but knew nothing about homosexuality, so she educated herself in order to support her grandson. She visited the local library and borrowed a book on homosexuality. On a visit to her doctor, she collected every brochure on HIV and AIDS, stuffed them into her handbag and went home to study. Regular family dinners became her way of showing support. Not bad for someone of her generation.

1992

In February Tony donned leathers and set off to Mardi Gras to join his fellow revellers as they gathered to parade, wave and blow kisses to the cheering crowds lining the route along Oxford Street through Taylor Square then towards Moore Park, where well-earned respite awaited. Sitting nearby on a hay bale and tugging at her hands was Julie Bates, a fellow activist Tony held in high esteem.

Articulate and feisty, Julie, a founding member of the Australian

Prostitutes' Collective, had successfully challenged authorities on behalf of two of society's most downtrodden groups, sex workers and intravenous drug users, to have condom use made mandatory in brothels and a needle-exchange program made available to drug users, causes that to Tony were as significant as ACT UP's. Years later Julie would be recognised for her courage and achievements with an Order of Australia medal.

'Whatever are you doing, Julie?' asked Tony, joining her on the hay bale and looking down at her clenched hands. 'Can I help?'

'Tony! Thank God it's you! Do I need some help? You bet I do. I've gone and handcuffed myself and I can't find the key.'

Tony exploded into laughter. 'How on earth did you manage to do that, Julie? And why?'

'I was planning to get even with my boyfriend tonight,' she sighed. 'He's been a bit naughty lately so I decided I'd handcuff him, rein him in, so to speak. I thought I'd try them out on myself first but now I can't get them off and I've lost the key. Got any ideas?'

'Plenty,' replied Tony, abandoning his plan to finish the march. 'Let's get started with a couple of sex shops. You used to joke about wanting to spend a night with me so now's our chance.'

They laughed their way back up Oxford Street on a tour of adult shops and anywhere else Tony thought a handcuff expert might be lurking, except the police station.

'It was a fun night,' Julie recalled, many years later. 'When The Toolshed and Bondage Bazaar couldn't help, we tried pubs and dance clubs. We'd have a drink or two then leave with me still cuffed. Eventually Tony decided to visit a "leathermen's" hangout in some back lane off Oxford Street, and someone there found a box of keys so I finally got freed. We missed some of the parade but we had a ball at the after party.'

When I told her about my plan to write his story she suggested, 'The best title for a book about Tony would have to be *Take No Bullshit*.'

During the year 1992, in Australia, 1027 people test HIV-positive, 836 are diagnosed with AIDS and there are 597 deaths.

The Albion Centre, *A HIV/AIDS Timeline*

Acacius (Stigmata) – Portrait of Tony Carden, AñA Wojak, 1991.

Chapter 17

Caught!

> The AIDS age has brought many deaths for gay men everywhere. We have all lost so many friends, acquaintances and lovers that our imaginations and psyches have had to resolve massive amounts of grief, similar in magnitude to a major war. Meanwhile, society carries on, unaware.
>
> Tony's journal, 1995

1992

A bonus of visiting Darlinghurst was the opportunity to pick up a copy of the *Sydney Star Observer*. It catered to Sydney's gay community, providing finger-on-the-pulse updates on everything HIV/AIDS; news from community-based organisations and state and federal politics; reviews of theatre, cinema and the art scene. Nothing newsy, gossipy or significant was missed and every reader had their opportunity to express their opinion via the letters page. Gradually throughout the '80s and '90s its obituaries section grew from a single column to a page, then to several pages as the grim reaper bowled over more and more victims. In a bad week there could be more than twenty obituaries. Living in the area, attending the same clinics, pharmacies and supermarkets, and meeting at dance parties meant fellow residents weren't strangers, they were friends, and the enormity of their loss was impossible to fathom. Ross Duffin recalled, 'Every week when *The Star* came out, we'd sit down for our lunch break, look over the headlines, read the obituaries, have a good cry as we remembered the friends we'd lost, then shake our heads and get back to work.'

'It's like fighting in a war,' Tony told me. 'People who were with you yesterday can be gone tomorrow and you don't know who'll be next. You can't imagine how it hurts.'

* * *

One night, under cover of darkness, Bruce and Tony crept furtively along Darlinghurst's back alleys towards the office of the gay magazine *Campaign*, up-collared dark coats concealing not only their faces but their weapons: a can of red spray-paint, 'borrowed' from ACT UP's storeroom. Their mission: social justice.

When they arrived they scanned the surrounds. All quiet. No observers. Tony shook the spray can and opened the lid. In bold letters, he wrote, 'Campaign' across the wall, then 'Racist', while Bruce, in his best hand, wrote 'Pigs' at the end.

'Done!' said Tony, standing back to admire their artistry. 'Quick, Bruce. Put the lid on and we'll get going.'

'You're going nowhere, you louts. You're under arrest,' an authoritarian voice boomed from the darkness. Proud of his 'catch', their captor marched them unceremoniously up the lane and around the corner to the police station.

I learnt about the escapade by accident. I'd dropped by Mary's retirement village to pay her a visit, to find her reading, much to my surprise, the *Sydney Star Observer*.

'My neighbour lent me this paper to read an article about her son Peter. He's a solicitor and he's spending his spare time helping the gay community in Darlinghurst. Perhaps Tony might know him. Here, take a look.'

I read the article then flicked the page over to be confronted by a photo of Tony and Bruce under the headline: 'TWO MEN

ARRESTED FOR SPRAYING GRAFFITI ON CAMPAIGN'S BUILDING'. I hastily folded the paper and handed it back, hoping Mary wouldn't look further. I didn't mention it to Tony, but he told me later what had happened. A homophobic, racist letter about Asian gay men had been published in *Campaign* magazine, causing a furore among both Sydney's Asian and gay communities. When a retraction and apology were demanded, the magazine's editor had refused, claiming the right to free speech.

The two graffitists appeared in the local court before an unsympathetic magistrate, who found them guilty of causing malicious damage and fined each of them $300, plus $100 in compensation, which their sympathetic 'other family' – the local gay community – promptly paid. The *Sydney Star Observer* made no secret of their predicament and the news was soon the buzz of Oxford Street.

Philanthropist and barrister David Buchanan immediately lodged an appeal on their behalf.

Tony and Bruce Brown (right), photographed in Darlinghurst, 1993.
Photo: Brett Monaghan, *Sydney Star Observer*

'The letter was plainly offensive,' declared the judge who presided over the appeal, 'Each appellant acted out of motives to be applauded, namely anti-racism. Neither has a criminal record and both men are in very poor health. With regard to their motivation and previous good character, I dismiss the charges.'

Caught, convicted, then appealed, off the hook! Their other family welcomed the reprieve of their brave sons.

The judge wasn't wrong about Tony's health. The saga had taken its toll.

'I'm feeling tired. I'd like a few days at Avalon for some home-cooked food and a few dips in the ocean to help me get over all this,' Tony said as we sat on the balcony at the Frisco Hotel two weeks later.

When we arrived, instead of taking his blue suitcase to the downstairs bedroom as he usually did, he was so tired that he dumped it on the bed in the room beside mine and lay down. He'd developed a cough as well, and the next night when he skipped his bedtime shower, something he insisted ensured a good night's sleep, I was concerned. He tossed and turned and coughed incessantly until finally I went to his room to find him confused and sweating profusely. His burning forehead and bloodshot eyes made up my mind.

'Tony, get up and I'll help you into your dressing-gown. We're going to hospital.'

It was four in the morning. He protested but lacked the will to resist as I half dragged him through the garden and up to the car. Presuming his illness was probably AIDS-related, we set off for the hour-long trip to St Vincent's, Tony lying back in the passenger seat, breathing in noisy gasps. Heart racing, I put my foot down and headed towards the city.

'I need a wheelchair. I have a very sick patient in the car,' I panted to the emergency department nurse. They triaged the breathless Tony as urgent and promptly administered oxygen while two orderlies lifted him onto a trolley. The doctor arrived, applied his stethoscope and announced, 'It sounds like pneumonia.'

It's happening again, I thought in disbelief, as a nurse wheeled Tony's trolley down the corridor past other AIDS patients, each secreted in a tiny cubicle. She parked him in a doorless alcove at the far end of the emergency department that was actually a broom cupboard, leaving him breathing noisily through an oxygen mask and me speechless and with no chair.

'There are no beds in the AIDS ward so he'll have to stay here. We'll X-ray his chest tomorrow.'

So here was Tony, living out the very scenario he and Clover had been warning politicians about for months: that AIDS patients in emergency needed treatment and drugs that could only be prescribed by specialist AIDS doctors, otherwise they would die.

I called Bruce.

'Pneumonia? If it's PCP it's urgent. He needs treatment straight away. I'll be there as fast as I can.'

Relieved to see his friend, Tony tugged at the mask in an effort to greet him. Bruce's fury was obvious. He headed straight to the payphone and called Clover, who in turn called the state Minister for Health, John Hannaford, to insist that unless six extra beds were provided for the AIDS ward immediately, lives would be lost, and their loss would be directly attributable to his inaction. She requested that he visit the emergency department that night as a matter of urgency. Otherwise the story would hit the papers.

Hannaford arrived to witness the debacle and, as a temporary fix, arranged a shuffle whereby AIDS patients who were stable were taken across the street to the palliative care hospice, to make beds available for Tony and others like him critically ill. But for Clover, Tony and ACT UP, it was only a stopgap measure.

* * *

Green Park, opposite St Vincent's, was living up to its name on a sunny, blue-sky day as I crossed Victoria Street to visit Tony in the

AIDS ward. I entered the hospital through a wide sandstone archway, crossed a spacious, blue-curtained room furnished with leather chairs, and took a walkway at the far end to a tall red-brick building behind the main hospital. From there a lift delivered me to Ward 17 South.

Nothing could have prepared me for the shock of my first visit to an AIDS ward. I gazed in disbelief into doorless wards where rows of desperately ill men, mostly young, emaciated and pale, many with the dark-purple weals of KS across their faces, arms and legs, lay on narrow beds. I glanced at each bed searching for Tony, forcing smiles at those who looked back at me, some little older than teenagers. Then I spotted him in a corner bed, lying back on raised pillows. I put my flowers and fruit on his bedside table and hugged him.

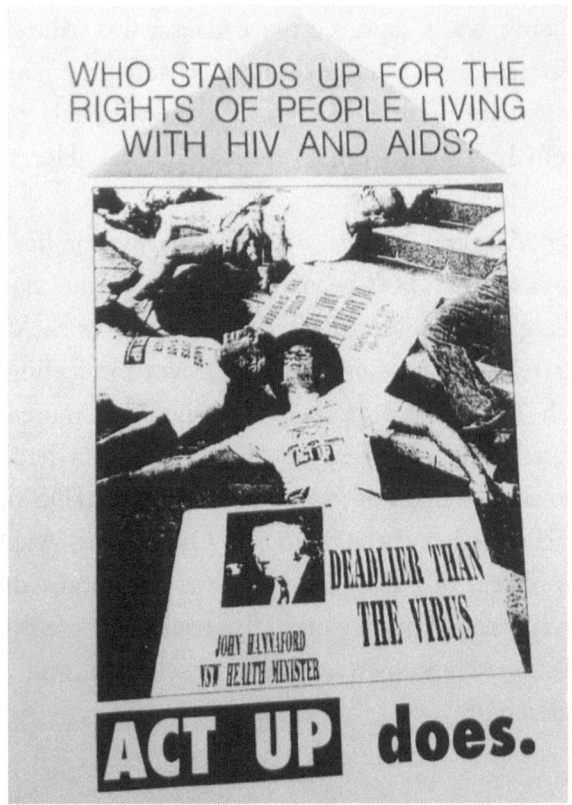

ACT UP poster, 1991.

'I've got PCP pneumonia but the good news is we have a new drug for it now, thanks to ACT UP. All our hard work has paid off. It's called Bactrim and it's pretty strong. It'll take my body a while to get used to it, so it could be a few more weeks before I can tolerate the full dose, but it's a lifesaver.'

I drew up a chair, realising that without Bruce's and Clover's intervention he would probably have died. I'd read that PCP (pneumocystis pneumonia) was a major cause of death for people with AIDS, silently grateful that Australia now had treatment for it.

Tony was very worried about his dog Caesar, who'd escaped from the yard of the friend who'd been minding him. Both the *Sydney Star Observer* and *The Sydney Morning Herald* had been alerting Darlinghurst residents to keep a lookout for a hospitalised man's dog, but despite being nearly captured twice Caesar was still on the run.

As we chatted, a middle-aged lady, her soft-grey fringe framing hazel eyes, wearing a grey skirt and a navy jacket, rosary beads dangling from her waist, walked over to join us. Her warm smile beamed kindness and sincerity.

'I'm Sister Margaret Mines,' she said, offering me her hand. 'You must be Tony's mother. He's been a very sick boy, you know.'

'Sister Margaret's wonderful,' Tony told me after she'd gone. 'She never spouts religion but somehow she leaves me feeling spiritually uplifted. If she's a typical nun, then there should be more like her.'

There were. When Premier Joh Bjelke-Petersen had refused to accept Queensland's share of federal government AIDS funding, the money was channelled through to the Queensland AIDS Council through the Sisters of Mercy at the Mater Hospital, who hid it in bags and envelopes and matter-of-factly ensured its safe delivery. They became affectionately known as 'the most cheerful and altruistic of money launderers'.[18]

---

18 To quote Neil Blewett.

Medically acquired HIV: $50,000 payout

The state government is preparing to announce that people who acquired HIV medically will receive a one-off, $50,000 payment as part of a $16 million compensation package being finalised by Cabinet.

An estimated 350 people in NSW have acquired the virus through blood transfusions and blood products.

Leading AIDS organisations, including the AIDS Council of NSW, claim that to compensate people who have acquired HIV medically, and not those who contracted it through sexual contact or the use of needles, is to create 'guilty' and 'innocent' sufferers.

Under the deal, relatives of those who acquired HIV medically but have since died would be eligible for a $10,000 payment.

The Sydney Morning Herald, 28 February 1992

Chapter 18

One Hundred Beds and 907 White Carnations

I bucked up and pretended nothing unusual was happening. After all, no-one likes a whinger.

Tony's journal, 1995

1992

Relieved to be back at home in Woolloomooloo, Tony gradually regained his strength. He struggled not only with rehabilitation, but with grief as well. While he was in hospital, Caesar had been hit and killed by a car.

Memories of the young men who'd been lined up beside him on trolleys in the emergency department's hallway needled away at Tony, a constant reminder of what needed to be done. It was now over a year since he and Clover had first begun lobbying for more AIDS beds, yet despite ever-increasing numbers of life-and-death emergencies, little had changed, and the situation was now dire. Grateful to have been one of the lucky ones to be admitted into an AIDS ward, he was still haunted by its coldness and impersonality. He'd seen young gay men there with no family to visit or comfort them, facing lonely, bleak deaths. He decided to take action with a gleam in his eye as an idea for a new campaign began to stir.

To boost his spirits he adopted a perky, white fluffy Bichon Frisé puppy. 'Biche' became Caesar's successor.

At the next ACT UP meeting, a familiar voice greeted members from the back of the hall, announcing an absent warrior's return. 'Please don't get up anyone, it's only me.'

They got up, of course, turned and slow-clapped Tony to his seat to calls of 'Better late than never!' and 'What some people will do to get attention'.

With the Pharmaceutical Benefits Scheme amended and the drug supply problem resolved, ACT UP's main mission was now fulfilled and their meetings had become more relaxed. The proactive zest of earlier days had dwindled, illness having weakened some and others having been lost to AIDS. But the *Sydney Star Observer*'s article about Tony's recent close shave in emergency and the revelation of how desperate the AIDS beds situation had become were causing their activism nerve to twitch.

Tony added to their disquiet. 'Clover's been working for months on this health minister and he keeps saying "Yes, yes, yes," but never delivers,' Tony complained. 'It's a political ploy he uses to avoid a confrontation. That way he gets away with doing nothing. I reckon this guy's time is up. What I experienced in emergency last month was the last straw. I could easily have died there and others already have, so let's do something that will make John Hannaford sit up and take notice. Let's show him what an AIDS ward should really look like.'

He'd been itching for another large-scale production and already had a vision of how it might look. ACT UP's best strategists got busy and the 'MORE AIDS BEDS NOW' campaign got under way. What they dreamt up was pure theatre. Enthusiasm spread throughout the meeting room as they began to flesh out the bones of the plan, members interjecting with suggestions, their keenness heightening with their anticipation of the new challenge. The vote to go ahead was unanimous.

Kirsty Machon, proved to be exactly the shot in the arm ACT UP needed for this new challenge. Calmly applying her down-to-earth organisational skills, Kirsty came straight to the point. 'We should build up some momentum before we get going,' she suggested. 'Let's hit *The Star* first with letters of complaint about the beds crisis and statements from some of the patients who've been given the trolleys-in-the-corridor treatment.'

'It's important we copy every letter and statement to the minister,' Claude insisted. 'I'll design a poster calling for volunteers and I'll also make sure they're well-displayed because if we're going to stage a one-hundred-bed ward, we'll need one hundred patients, and doctors and nurses as well.'

ACT UP poster for the '100 Beds' demonstration, 1992.

After a busy week they met again to report on their progress.

'Bruce and I took a trip out to Denistone last week to check out Hannaford's street,' said Tony. 'There's no front fence and his front lawn's flat so we can spill over onto the nature strip for our speeches. And if our banner's high up behind the stage, both it and the speakers will catch the afternoon sun. The press photographers' cameras will have perfect lighting while the journos are recording the speeches.'

Tony's batteries were being recharged by a remedy more potent than any drug. 'We'll need someone to organise the props,' he continued, winking at Kirsty, whose contacts were widespread. 'Hopefully some of our hospital contacts will agree to lend a hand.'

Kirsty smiled and nodded.

* * *

In the early hours of the morning of 24 January 1992, a large truck backed down the ramp into the basement of St Vincent's, where the roller door had conveniently been unlocked. One hundred disassembled hospital beds and mattresses were silently loaded onto the truck along with bags of medical equipment, sheets and uniforms. Later that same morning a large crowd set off from Denistone Station, many with pyjamas in backpacks, heading for John Hannaford's house, chanting the slogan 'AIDS Beds Now' and bearing posters that said the same. Police re-directed traffic and cameramen were there to capture the desperation and determination on the marchers' faces.

As they rounded the corner of his street, they beheld a makeshift hospital ward: the lawn and nature strip were covered in rows of white-blanketed beds, a drip-stand beside each. White-coated 'doctors', stethoscopes draped around their necks, were adjusting the drips, while uniformed 'nurses' went from bed to bed tucking in each 'patient' as he or she hastily clambered into pyjamas. A raised platform backed by a huge red, white and black 'AIDS BEDS NOW' banner served as a stage. Peeking through the curtains of the house were four pairs of amazed eyes watching the performance – the wife and family of Health Minister Hannaford. Bruce and Tony stood awaiting the arrival of journalists and photographers before presenting their speeches.

'We are here today to protest the critical shortage of beds in HIV/AIDS wards in Sydney hospitals,' Bruce told the crowd. 'It is now a public emergency and the inaction of the NSW Health Minister John Hannaford has also made it a public disgrace. I am living with AIDS. Last year when I was very seriously ill my doctor told me I needed to be admitted to St Vincent's. Then he called me back to say, "Don't come. The ward is full and if you come to the hospital you'll be the fifth person with AIDS in the queue in casualty. All I can do is visit you at home and do the best I can." Many have died for lack of a bed and I might have, too. Where, Minister, are the beds?'

Tony spoke next, describing his near-death experience, and reading statements from several others who'd suffered similarly. From curtain-call to epilogue the performance ran for twenty-five minutes, concluding with cheers and wild applause from the crowd. TV, newspaper and radio coverage continued through the week followed by a flow of public feedback. Someone had left Minister Hannaford a calling card: etched across his green lawn in dead grass the word 'MURDERER'.

Tony's request two weeks later for an interview with John Hannaford was granted. Understandably, the meeting wasn't warm, but the gauntlet had been firmly laid down. In April St Vincent's gained six new AIDS beds. Emboldened, Tony battled on alongside Clover for further funding and turned his theatrical bent towards two more protests before the year was out. Pushing illness to the background and elated by his return to the stage, he compensated for his lack of energy with passion and determination.

* * *

The fifth National AIDS Conference was to be held at Darling Harbour in November. The list of speakers was impressive: medical experts to present the latest research findings; pharmaceutical companies to reveal the progress they'd made with anti-virals and a myriad of other AIDS drugs; and representatives from government AIDS organisations.

With nothing new on their agenda, ACT UP's August meeting was an informal get-together of core members. As they studied the impressive line-up of 'experts' on the conference program, they noticed that one group was clearly missing.

'They've done it again!' Bruce complained. 'Not one of us has been invited to speak. It's a repeat of Tasmania in 1988. Remember? They'll be speaking ABOUT us but not WITH us again. They're acting as though we're invisible.'

'Remember the protest at that conference?' Kirsty reminded them. 'No-one said a word. They just wore badges and raised banners, but their silent messages came through loud and clear. We don't need to be disruptive. Let's plan another silent protest.'

So with some 'inside' help they acquired fifteen press passes and planned a silent stage takeover.

As the last speaker of the day was introducing her topic, fifteen 'delegates' rose from the audience and moved quietly towards the stage, where earlier Kirsty had surreptitiously placed five florists' boxes. In single file, each took a long-stemmed white carnation, mounted the steps, walked towards the speaker and gently stooped to place their carnation at her feet. Making no eye contact, they glided across the stage, descended the steps at the other side, gathered another carnation and returned in a stream, repeating the procedure until the floor of the stage had been transformed into a sea of white, lapping around the speaker's feet, marooning her like a lonely rock within a fragrant sea. They returned to their seats, two remaining to unfurl a banner proclaiming:

IN MEMORY OF 907 AUSTRALIANS WHO'VE DIED FROM AIDS DURING THE PAST YEAR

* * *

World AIDS Day, a World Health Organization initiative to raise public awareness of the pandemic and to mourn those who have died, is observed annually worldwide on 1st December. ACT UP's members were appalled to discover that once again no HIV-positive people were to be invited to speak at Sydney's official 1992 World AIDS Day ceremony in Pitt Street, so they decided they'd invite themselves.

As the Master of Ceremonies was discussing the challenges of the ongoing epidemic, Tony called out, 'We're on now.'

Red T-shirted protestors arose from the audience like poppies sprouting from a field and headed towards the stage through a swarm of red balloons that swirled up from below, released by ACT UP accomplices. Tony, dapper in black trousers, white shirt and red bowtie, sprang up the steps on one side of the stage as singer Judi Connelli approached from the other. Handing him the microphone, she smiled, and offered him her hand in invitation. 'Sing with me, darling,' she said.

Tony's New York singing lessons proved their worth that day as his rich tenor tones merged with Judi's lilting soprano melody in a rousing performance of the AIDS memorial anthem accompanied by the band. The captivated audience, intrigued by the stage-crasher's aplomb, cheered when he stepped forward to address them.

'Good morning, everyone. My name's Tony Carden and I have AIDS. Last year fifteen million people worldwide were living with HIV and over one thousand of those were Australians. Last year eight hundred and thirty-six of us progressed from being HIV-positive to having full-blown AIDS and seven hundred died. This year's toll will be even higher and every year it will continue to increase until there's a cure so eventually every one of you will be touched in some way by this disease. The theme of this year's World AIDS Day is "Community Commitment" and if we're going to turn those numbers around, we'll all need to pull together.'

As he left the stage, members of the audience crowded forward to commend him, among them a woman with dark bobbed hair, her troubled eyes meeting his as she shook his hand.

'That was very moving, Tony. I live in Woolloomooloo and it's breaking my heart to see so many of my friends getting sick and struggling to cope. There must be something I can do. I can't just stand by and watch.'

As they chatted Tony sensed he'd made a new friend.

'Oh, by the way, Tony, I'm Carole Ann King.'

The International AIDS Candlelight Memorial is one of the world's oldest and largest grassroots mobilisation campaigns and takes place annually every third Sunday in May.

It began in San Francisco in 1983 to inspire people living with HIV/AIDS in other countries to bring HIV into the light and for communities and national leaders to foster support and lead people into action.

Since that day the AIDS Candlelight Memorial has brought together people in every region of the world to honour those lost to AIDS and support people living with HIV.

Sydney Candlelight Memorial

Chapter 19

Someone's Uncle

> I feel very happy that I was able to be involved in my brother's fight for the things that most of us take for granted – the right to be treated with respect, equality and dignity.
>
> Carolyn Carden, Tony's sister, from her *Warrior Blood* profile

1993

As daylight faded, pale stars began to glow in a cloudless sky and candles flickered to life as over 2,000 people wound their way along the streets of Sydney towards Hyde Park for the International Candlelight Memorial. When they arrived, they spread blankets on the grass and opened picnic baskets as children frolicked beneath the fig trees and lights from the stage shone down onto a grassy candlelit 'carpet'. Each year the list of those Australians who'd lost their lives to AIDS was growing longer, and the number of people who considered it an honour to read out their names increased.

As Tony took his place in the line of readers, he noticed a familiar face behind him. 'Hello, Carole Ann. I see you're living up to your word,' he remarked. 'You couldn't have chosen a better way to support us.'

'Actually, I've got an idea about something else I'd like to do,' she said.

'Let's talk,' replied Tony.

* * *

Living in Woolloomooloo put Carole Ann within walking distance of Oxford Street, once a hub of bright lights and hedonism, now a battlefield for Australia's highest concentration of AIDS cases. She'd attended funeral after funeral for some of her dearest and closest friends and had witnessed too much grief. She wanted to bring some joy back into the community so she decided to throw a party.

The Lizard Lounge, upstairs in Oxford Street's Exchange Hotel, could accommodate a couple of hundred people, had a stage and a well-equipped kitchen and was very accessible. Carole Ann decided its worn interior could easily be dressed up with decorations to look festive, so she took the plunge and booked it. Now came the biggest challenge of the exercise: how to fund it. She set to work asking potential sponsors to donate food and beverages. 'No' was unacceptable to Carole Ann, and soon sponsors and volunteers were emerging from all parts of Sydney. Musicians and drag queens offered their entertainment. Carole Ann's party soon became the talk of the town. She imposed only one condition: 'We're not going to talk about death, dying, funerals or wakes. We're going to be living with AIDS, not dying from AIDS.'

The Lizard Lounge was in cabaret mode when the big day arrived, with soft lighting, balloons and streamers. Tables were set with tablecloths, flowers and bowls of nuts. The aroma of freshly baked ham and barbecued chicken greeted guests on arrival. Twenty excited volunteers wearing aprons and plastic gloves who'd spent the morning peeling, slicing, cooking and carving handed around drinks, dips, cheese and crackers or took up positions as servers behind the smorgasbord as Carole Ann, not only the gracious hostess but also a competent people-manager, mingled among almost ninety guests, many of whom could no longer afford such outings. After second helpings and dessert, a drum rolled, lights dimmed and a spotlight flashed off a tiara set atop coiffured auburn ringlets. In a flurry of feathers, Carlotta, queen of drag, glided onto the stage, her skin-tight scarlet satin dress with plunging neckline accentuating her sensuous curves. For four hours,

AIDS was forgotten. Showering their hostess with hugs and kisses, departing guests pleaded, 'Could we do it again some time, Carole Ann? Please?'

Carole Ann did indeed do it again. In fact, her Luncheon Club ran every week for the next fourteen years. Food leftover from each luncheon was donated along with everyday items such as soap and toothpaste to impoverished Darlinghurst AIDS patients struggling to exist on small pensions. To the gay and lesbian community, Carole Ann became known as an angel, even a saint. When she was nominated for a national award she declined it, preferring not to be acknowledged for her achievements. Such was her humility.

'And to think,' Carole Ann later remarked to Tony, 'a lot of your friends thought that because I was straight, I was probably a spy. How's that for discrimination?'

* * *

One afternoon Tony and I sat soaking up the sun and enjoying a fish and chips lunch on the upstairs verandah of the Frisco. As we chatted, I realised he'd changed; there'd been clues but I hadn't connected them: the short walk from the Crystal House to the Frisco for lunch had taken longer today than a year ago; and he could no longer scale the steep, old wooden staircase to the verandah two steps at a time; his body had become leaner, more angular, his cheekbones more prominent, his hair thinner; his eye-twinkles were there, lively as ever, but his eyes looked larger, deeper-set beneath their boldly arched brows.

'We're working on a new anti-discrimination campaign,' he remarked, popping a chip into his mouth and crunching it. 'That grim reaper campaign scared the living daylights out of everyone. The stigma of being HIV-positive is deterring people from coming forward to be tested and that's only spreading the disease more so we're hoping this campaign will change all that. We want to show people that it's okay to socialise with someone who has AIDS, that we're not a threat, that having lunch or a cup of coffee with us or hugging us is perfectly safe.'

'That sounds like a good idea, Tony,' I reflected, 'because lots of people are genuinely afraid.'

A new government-funded anti-discrimination campaign to supersede the grim reaper campaign was being planned and Tony was to be part of it, along with Lynna and Jamie, her two-year-old son.

The concept was based on research that had revealed something significant: people who knew someone with HIV/AIDS were far less likely to discriminate than those who didn't. This revelation was vital. It supported what had been suspected earlier: that when someone in the public eye, like Peter Allen, died of the disease, greater empathy and increased acceptance were felt within the community. This same phenomenon had been seen in the US following Rock Hudson's death from AIDS. So this time, instead of actors, they'd use real people with AIDS in everyday situations to present a campaign based on honesty and authenticity.

Frances Dart, the casting agent, later recalled, 'Tony came along with his dog, fresh from the dog psychologist, and made a huge impression on us all. He was totally outrageous and had a wicked sense of humour. He had great charisma and everyone took to him immediately.'

The campaign appeared Australia-wide in print and on television in early January 1993. The first sequence focused on three scenarios: 'someone's friend' showed two friends in a restaurant, talking and laughing over a shared bottle of wine; 'someone's sister' had a woman sitting on a couch with her brother, chatting and eating fish and chips from the same packet; and 'someone's boss' depicted someone in a white lab coat instructing an employee on the art of jewellery-making.

Tony appeared in a second sequence as 'someone's uncle', which had him strolling along the wharf at Careel Bay with Lynna carrying Jamie. Jamie looks up at his uncle and chuckles as pelicans soar overhead in a sunny sky; 'someone's husband' depicted a man ambling along a bush

I Don't Want to Talk About It

Promotional photo for AIDS anti-discrimination campaign featuring Tony with his sister Lynna and nephew Jamie.
Sydney Star Observer, 1993

track, hand in hand with his wife, both admiring the wildflowers; in 'someone's partner' a same-sex couple are poring over photos in an album and reminiscing. A third sequence included 'someone's child', 'someone's workmate' and 'someone's son'. The caption below each scenario read: 'Ordinary people with something in common: They're all HIV-positive. AIDS is a virus. It doesn't discriminate, people do.' In the background a voice softly sings to a lilting melody, 'All I want is to live each moment, free from hatred, free from hurt.'

Within a few days of the ads appearing my phone began to ring with calls from friends, neighbours, even people I'd taught, all asking, 'Why didn't you tell us about Tony?' The calls continued for days.

I explained that Tony had initially preferred to keep his HIV status quiet because he didn't want to be treated as though he was dying.

On reflection, had I been honest I'd have owned up to the other reason: I wanted to avoid the discrimination I feared would deter my students and damage my business. Also, I wanted to protect myself from the insensitivity of the world around me.

* * *

The conference room of the Marriott Hotel opposite Hyde Park in Sydney was buzzing. It was the afternoon of the campaign's official launch. The Minister for Health formally opened the campaign, praising his government's proactivity in tackling discrimination. Then came the campaign director, who gave credit to Tony. 'He's a courageous man who has worked throughout the years of the epidemic with ACT UP, towards bettering the lives of all Australians with HIV/AIDS. Ladies and gentlemen, Tony Carden.'

Tony, debonair in silky grey suit, green shirt and black-and-yellow tie, stepped up to the podium, smiling as he jested with the audience before launching into his speech:

> My name is Tony Carden and I am HIV positive. So are my friends here involved in the campaign. All of us in the campaign have taken the courageous stand of revealing our HIV status before the entire nation in the hope that it will put to an end HIV/AIDS discrimination ... Discrimination takes many forms, ranging from small things such as breaches of confidentiality to extreme actions such as violence against individuals and groups. While not everybody with HIV experiences discrimination, we *all* fear it. People isolate themselves from support systems and treatments that can enhance their lives. I know, because I did so for four years.
>
> I would like to give the Australian public a challenge that each one of us has embraced: to bring to an end discrimination towards people who are HIV-positive in Australia; to

acknowledge and fight discrimination in all its forms in our society and eliminate it forever.

The campaign had cast a humane light on the tragedy of AIDS. (Feedback from the public and the gay community was so positive that later in the year the campaign was repeated.)

But it didn't end there. With discrimination, homosexuality and AIDS now in the forefront of people's minds, the time was ripe for Clover to make her move.

GAY RIGHTS?
UNDER GOD'S LAW THE ONLY
'RIGHTS' GAYS HAVE IS THE RIGHT TO DIE
(LEVITICUS 20:13)
    Bumper sticker for sale at the Royal Agricultural Society's
      Sydney Showground Antique Gun Fair, 1992

Chapter 20

The Bill

> New legislation will make it illegal to discriminate against people with HIV in health, education, accommodation, insurance, superannuation, employment, law, public services – and autopsy. Yes, people are even being discriminated against when they are dead.
>
> Tony's speech at the Anti-Discrimination Campaign launch, 1993

1993

For three years, Clover and Tony had worked together to tackle the challenges of living with HIV/AIDS. They'd hosted regular AIDS forums at Parliament House, inviting representatives from AIDS organisations and the gay community to come together to air their concerns. Whether those concerns were about dentistry, housing or employment, the overarching factor behind every one was discrimination.

Two years had passed since ACT UP's 'Storm the ADB' protest and it constantly rankled with Tony that after such wide publicisation of the demonstration and despite Clover's continual political demands, nothing had been achieved.

'Dealing with discrimination is the Anti-Discrimination Board's responsibility. It's their business,' he remonstrated one steamy summer afternoon at the Frisco. 'And, as far as the gay community and AIDS are concerned, it's unfinished business.'

Now, with the new anti-discrimination campaign fresh in everyone's minds, and Clover agitating in the wings, the ADB could stall no longer. Even Brian Howe, the federal Minister for Health, had accepted that the time was right to take up the gauntlet. Altruism or not, politically, it was timely. He organised a research program into the extent of discrimination in the community: where it was greatest, which groups of people were most likely to discriminate, and what factors triggered it. The results may have surprised the government, but not Tony or Clover. It was revealed that HIV/AIDS discrimination was rife throughout the entire nation and at its very worst in rural areas, where suicides had increased significantly since the advent of HIV. Even so, the Anti-Discrimination Board, like a bear in hibernation, continued to procrastinate, so Clover, despite the antagonism she knew she would incite, took action.

In February she presented her Anti-Discrimination (Homosexual Vilification) Amendment Bill to the New South Wales Parliament. The response was varied: empathetic members were enthusiastic, stiff-shirted conservatives uneasy, while Fred Nile and his Christian Democratic Party condemned it outright on religious grounds. The bill made it an offence to publicly incite hatred, serious contempt or ridicule of homosexual men or women. Irate, Fred argued: 'The homosexuals have already got everything they want. This bill would mean no-one could criticise their lifestyle.'

Exactly, Fred!

Posters began to appear around the city:

DEATH

PENALTY

for

HOMOSEXUALS

is

PRESCRIBED IN THE BIBLE

Clover's bill, introduced to parliament's Lower House in February, was duly debated, and ultimately passed in May. Tony was ecstatic.

'So far, so good – no hitches,' he told me. 'Clover's pure gold. I've been thinking for a while now about how we could thank her, the gay community, I mean. I'd like us to do something more personal than just send her some flowers and a thank you note. It needs to be something she'd really get a kick out of, and I've come up with a very exciting idea.'

He said no more, but from the glint in his eye, I knew it would be another of his grand productions.

The bill proceeded to the Upper House where, undermined by Fred, it was blocked at its second reading, which consigned it to a four-month-long hibernation until parliament was due to meet again in September. Should it be blocked once more, it would be doomed.

But the gay community were ready and determined not to allow this to happen. They'd been impressed by the huge turnout of almost twelve thousand supporters who had gathered at the last Candlelight Memorial, so perhaps they could be re-rallied to help save the bill? They began to plan.

* * *

Tony took advantage of the parliamentary break to start thinking about his 'Thank You, Clover' project. One morning he went to Clover's home in Redfern for a clandestine appointment with her husband, architect Peter Moore.

'Clover won't be back for hours,' Peter told Tony, inviting him inside the homey 1800s brick terrace house. 'I've had time to look through her wardrobe and I've found something I think would be perfect – it's a linen suit she wears in summer and photographs of her wearing it were in the media quite a few times last summer. If she starts looking for it, I'll just tell her it's at the drycleaner's.'

Peter produced a loose-fit, black-and-white patterned two-piece suit.

Tony was delighted. 'It's perfect, Peter. As soon as I can get hold of some matching fabric, I'll find a tailor who can copy it and then we'll be in business.'

In July, using an airline ticket paid for by his brother Phil, Tony headed to New York, with several close-up photographs of Clover in his blue suitcase. The theatrical wig-maker he consulted was delighted to fill an order for twenty dark curly wigs as per the photographs. With two weeks to fill while the wigs were being made, Tony caught up with old friends and enjoyed a few Broadway shows. He returned to Australia refreshed, re-inspired, and ready to join the protest against the bill's deferment.

* * *

In September 1993, outside the NSW Parliament House he joined two thousand banner-waving demonstrators to oppose the bill's blockage. Fred Nile's side proposed an amendment to expand religious exemptions that would allow the Church's followers alone to right to discriminate against people with HIV/AIDS, while the remainder of the community would be bound by the act.

'Ah, the misconceptions of religion,' lamented Tony.

Clover fought back and the bill struggled along its obstacle-strewn course for two more months until it emerged clear of impediments. When the time came to vote it into law, Tony was there. He rang me the following day.

'I arrived at Parliament House at two in the morning and I had to sit waiting for another two and a half hours, but it wasn't boring because who do you think came rolling in, in a wheelchair, wearing pyjamas?'

'I don't know. Who?' I queried.

'Fred Nile, of course! Old Fred's a bit of a showman, you know. Apparently, he's got some broken ribs.'

'You and I have had broken ribs but we didn't need wheelchairs, did we, Tony?'

'He probably thought it would get him some sympathy, you know: a poor injured man struggling to defend his rights. Oh well, you can't blame Fred for wanting to put his bit in, but his bit didn't count this time, because the bill was passed. Ha! Ha! Three cheers for Clover!'

Clover became the toast of the gay community and a headline in the following week's *Sydney Star Observer* reported: 'GAYS FREED OF FRED'.

It was time to celebrate so Tony and his friend Simon Hunt organised a revue at the Belvoir Street Theatre, engaging stars of music, song and comedy, who happily donated their time and expertise. With the theatre charging only a token fee, tickets were affordable, and the event became a profitable fundraiser for his tribute to Clover.

The passing of the bill into law should have ensured a high-note ending for 1993, but that was not to be, because in November Bruce died.

* * *

For people like Bruce and Tony, AIDS meant that they would spend the rest of their lives navigating unsurveyed territory. The only certainty was the final destination. Bruce's and Tony's journeys had been remarkably similar. Both had experienced the early years of the epidemic in America, Bruce in San Francisco, Tony in New York. They had become infected around the same time. Both had thrown their energy and talents into their activism. Both were stricken by the same three of many auto-immune diseases: PCP pneumonia, thrush (candidiasis) and retinitis. Bruce had told Lyle that if he ever lost his sight, the balance between the quality and quantity of his life would have tipped over.

Tony, on the other hand, rarely mentioned the possibility of losing his eyesight. Whatever his thoughts, he kept them to himself.

Bruce's 'quality:quantity of life' ratio was an idea shared by many with AIDS because it was at the very core of what tormented them most: without a timely cure, they knew their journey's end would be lingering, painful and, even worse, beyond their control. Most were young men in their twenties or thirties who believed, as do young men worldwide, in their own indestructibility, so when their illnesses ground ruthlessly on and they became aware of what lay ahead, many contemplated where their 'tipping point' fell. More than a few had attempted suicide, several unsuccessfully, a tragedy that brought pain not only to themselves but also to their loved ones.

The ethical debate over euthanasia was then and continues to be a very hot political potato, viewable from a range of perspectives: basic human rights, religion, the Hippocratic oath, the vulnerability of the elderly and the terminally ill.

But AIDS was affecting people *now* and the need for a solution was urgent. The Voluntary Euthanasia Society of New South Wales Inc. was contacted and with their help an information booklet was produced, available on application. The booklet was eagerly sought after by those with AIDS and their community and others who were toying with the idea of what they referred to as 'self-delivery'.

At only 35, Bruce asked three close friends including Lyle, all ACT UP activists, to be present on his final evening. Back then, under Australian law it was a criminal offence to assist a suicide, and the question of how Bruce had died remained unasked, but on his bedside table lay a bottle of pills.

Lyle later recounted at the premiere of his string quartet, *An AIDS Activist's Memoir in Music:* 'That no-one could be in the same room was as inhumane a thing as one human being could do to another – to force an already solitary death to also be lonely.'

'Bruce asked each of us to go into his bedroom one at a time to say goodbye. Before I left, Bruce carefully counted out the pills, swallowed them and said, 'Dear God, please don't let me throw up'. I knew then, because I didn't know before, that Bruce believed in God.'

The three friends waited through the night, barely speaking. They drank coffee and listened to music: Umberto Giordano's 'La Mamma Morta', an aria played in the movie *Philadelphia*; and Bach's Goldberg Variations . . .

In the morning they went into Bruce's bedroom and found him still sitting up with his head resting on his chest, suggesting that, hopefully, he'd died quickly. He was cold. They called the police, as they had planned to do, and an ambulance came to remove Bruce's body.

When Tony told me Bruce had died, he mentioned it only briefly, too casually, I thought, knowing how deeply it must have affected him. He made no reference to Bruce's 'self-delivery'; instead he reflected on the infamous plots they'd hatched together to unsettle the citizenry, especially the 'red paint' incident, and how, because they'd stood up for the rights of others, they'd gotten the better of the law. Then he picked up an envelope from the table and handed it to me.

'This is something that's very important to me. I want you to keep it in a safe place and have it ready if I ever get to the stage where I can no longer express my wishes. The goddamn Kaposi sarcoma is spreading inside me now and, despite the chemotherapy, eventually it will reach my brain. When that happens, I'll probably get dementia, because that's what often happens with KS. Don't be upset. I've already seen it happen to some of my friends so I know what to expect. That's AIDS. When or if that happens, Lezzles, this letter will tell you and Phil, and the doctors who'll be looking after me, how I wish to be treated at the end of my life. I'll give Phil a copy so you two will both know about it.'

Tears choked my throat. I couldn't answer, so I breathed deeply before replying softly, 'Tony, you can rest assured that if ever that happens we'll follow your wishes to the letter, I promise, but let's hope they find a cure before then.'

He smiled, but there was sadness in his eyes.

Before I decided where to put the letter for safekeeping, I read it. Both he and Bruce, despite having so much in common, including their belief in God, had arrived at very different choices. Tony's letter left no doubt about his wishes: he wanted to be allowed to die naturally; he didn't want his life to be ended prematurely; he wanted every comfort that could be provided to ease his suffering. Self-delivery was not an option for Tony.

Apologising to the '78ers, Darren Goodsir, editor-in-chief of *The Sydney Morning Herald* said:

'In 1978 *The Sydney Morning Herald* reported the names, addresses and professions of people arrested during public protests to advance gay rights.

We acknowledge and apologise for the hurt and suffering that reporting caused. It would never happen today.'

Steve Warren, a '78er said:

'The apology has been a long time coming. It means a lot to the '78ers. We understand it was practice at the time but it hurt. Some '78ers lost jobs, lost family contact and, over the years, some even committed suicide.'

The Sydney Morning Herald, Thursday 25 February 2016

Chapter 21

Mardi Gras and Twenty Clovers

> This is a monumental moment for every Australian. Our campaign is the first of its kind in the world. We can be truly proud of the leadership role Australia is taking in the fight against HIV and its effect on the entire world.
>
> Tony's speech at the Anti-Discrimination Campaign launch, 1993

1994

Despite Fred's prayers, the morning of the Mardi Gras dawned promisingly clear. Oxford Street was in festive finery, with shops and cafes sparkling with tinsel, fairy lights draping branches and the rainbow flag waving high overhead.

Throughout the city an army of police were putting in place traffic diversions and barricades to hold back the expected hordes of onlookers, already beginning to arrive with folding chairs to claim premium positions. Aches and pains, disease and disability were put on hold as the marchers decorated floats, prepared costumes and added last-minute touch-ups to banners.

Tony had used Clover's Christmas party to bounce his plan for the 'Thank You, Clover' project off a few guests and they'd agreed to help and keep everything under wraps. A week later he and three collaborators had huddled around the table at the Crystal House to peruse the attendance lists for upcoming AIDS forums to find twenty suitable 'Clover look-alikes'.

Italian tailor Alfredo Bianchi,[19] delighted with his order for twenty ladies' suits, arrived one Saturday afternoon at the Crystal House, with measuring tape and notebook in hand. He'd probably looked twice when the twenty people included a number of young gay men, clad in singlets and jocks. With admirable aplomb he contained his relief that a lady's suit required no inside leg measurement.

'I'm aware that you don't allow send-ups of public figures,' Tony explained when he lodged his application for approval and funding with ACON. 'But this entry's definitely not a send-up. *It's a tribute*, and I can assure you it will be very complimentary to Clover because you and I know how much we all love her.'

For Clover, the Mardi Gras was her electorate's highlight event. Every year she looked forward to participating in it, in whatever way she was called on. When Tony rang to explain he'd already arranged a car for her and to invite her and Peter to the Crystal House at six for a pre-parade drink, she must have wondered what he was up to.

She was greeted in the back garden of the Crystal House by a cheering chorus from twenty people all wearing her suit, her hairstyle, her classic black court shoes, gold chains and drop earrings – even the same shade of bright lipstick. Glasses of champagne were passed around and one of the twenty raised a glass to toast her. It was only because of his voice that she recognised the immaculately clad and wigged Tony.

'To Clover, our wonderful member for Bligh and our very dear friend. Thank you for everything you've done for us. We love you, Clover.'

Clover later recalled, 'As we walked up to Oxford Street, old singleted Woolloomooloo men looked out their windows and shouted, "Have a good night, girls."'

---

19 Pseudonym.

Clover Moore, Tony and journalist Michael Glynn,
founder and editor of the *Sydney Star Observer*, Darlinghurst, 1995.

Seeing footage of the Mardi Gras's cheering crowds, sparsely clad marchers and high-coiffed queens in swirling dresses, I'd often been tempted to join the throngs of onlookers but until now I'd not succeeded so I was excited when Tony told me he'd arranged seats for Jane and me at the Quilt Project's office[20] in Oxford Street with a bird's-eye view of the action. We shared our privileged perch with emaciated young men with AIDS, once eager participants, now unable to join the fun, a sobering reminder that beneath the parade's gaiety lurked the harsh reality of AIDS.

As dusk settled over the city, a distant seismic rumble preceded the arrival of a horde of motorbikes, their engines revving to a full-throttled roar: the Dykes on Bikes. The fun had begun! Float after float

---

20 The Quilt Project was a volunteer-run organisation that guided people to create a memorial panel for someone who had died of AIDS. The panels were later put together to form the AIDS Memorial Quilt.

I Don't Want to Talk About It

Some of the twenty Clover Moore look-alikes in the
Mardi Gras tribute to Clover, Darlinghurst, 1994.

followed: drag queens in splendiferous creations of feathers, baubles and flashing lights, curls flowing, headdresses towering; marching uniformed Vancouver Mounties; rows of singing, scantily clad marchers and dancers; a Polynesian princess with palm-leaf-waving entourage; Wagga Wagga's 'Gay Family'; the Sisters of Perpetual Indulgence, brawny men in nuns' habits piously fingering their rosary beads: all in an endless celebration of merriment.

We saw not what Fred described as 'immoral and tantamount to indecent exposure', but svelte, semi-naked, gym-honed thirty-year-olds embodying the march's theme: 'We Are Family'.

Preceded by a marching drumroll was Tony's entry, 'Tribute to Clover Moore': a group of twenty gay and straight men and women all dressed Clover-style, marching behind the real Clover, who sat next to Peter in an open-top vehicle waving to crowds of her adoring constituents.

* * *

Amelia Menia and Tony had been friends since 1990 when she'd joined ACT UP to take up the torch on behalf of HIV-positive women. Amelia and her husband had been happily married for several years before discovering that not only was he HIV-positive, but, to their great anguish, he'd passed the virus on to her. Petite, with mischievous green eyes and a fluff of strawberry-blonde curls, Amelia could have been misread as fragile, but, like Tony, she was a warrior. Amelia lovingly nursed her husband throughout the years of his illness and then used her experience to help others.

Whenever Tony was hospitalised she'd visit him. On one occasion when Amelia arrived at Ward 17 South, I withdrew from Tony's bedside and retreated to the visitors' waiting room. Another visitor was there, perusing a magazine. I greeted her as I sat down, and when she smiled back, her green eyes and curly blonde hair suggested who she might be.

'Would you happen to be Amelia's mother?' I ventured.

'Yes, good guess. It's the hair that gives us away,' she laughed. 'I arrived yesterday from England so I'm still fairly jet-lagged. It's my first visit to Australia.'

'She'll be pleased you've come. How long are you planning to stay? By the way, I'm Lesley, Tony's mother.' My mind was ticking over, guessing she probably didn't know many Sydneysiders.

'Oh, I'll be staying here until the end.'

The end of what? I wondered, but before I could ask, she continued, 'Didn't you know Amelia has AIDS? She was very ill recently and came here to St Vincent's but they put her in the psychiatric ward because the AIDS ward doesn't have a women's section. They knew everything about psychiatry in the psychiatric ward, but not much about AIDS, and Amelia could tell they didn't want her there because they seemed quite nervous about handling her. So she discharged herself.'

Astonished, I frowned in dismay.

'Thank goodness Amelia has a good GP. And she's a woman, too, which is lucky for Amelia. She has arranged home care for her, which is just as well because Amelia has no intention of ever coming back here again.'

Like Bruce, Amelia had made her choice.

On the chosen afternoon, dressed in her cream lace wedding dress, light make-up on her face, she rested on a pile of pillows to await her guests.

Her mother later recalled, 'She looked quite angelic. Like a princess. I could hardly believe what was happening.'

Earlier in the afternoon, there'd been another guest, a brave and courageous friend who had set up Amelia's drip, placed a loaded syringe on her bedside table, tearfully hugged her, then left.

That afternoon, her mother and a few of her closest friends would share her last few hours with her. They toasted her life and their love for each other, shared memories, laughed a lot, cried a little, then left Amelia alone to squeeze the syringe's contents into the drip and lie back to await the drift to eternity.

Amelia and Bruce were two of possibly hundreds of Australians who chose to self-deliver during the AIDS epidemic. The need for secrecy meant we'll never know, but subsequent research suggested it may have accounted for a little over sixty-three per cent of AIDS deaths in Canada and Australia.

* * *

Keen to provide Tony some respite, Phil and Jenny sometimes took him to their home on the Hawkesbury River for a few days of spoiling and well-earned rest. Tony and his niece Phoebe, now four, adored each other. Her 'Uncle Max', the playful name Phoebe had derived from Tony's nickname 'Machiavelli', was happy to play and joke with her hour after hour.

'My niece Phoebe is special,' Tony wrote in his journal. 'She is a dancing fairy casting spells of laughter and loveliness, even without a wand. I have known her before when my spirit was carried in a different suitcase.'

One morning Phil, Jenny, Tony and Phoebe were tucking into a breakfast of pancakes when Keith called. He had devastating news. 'I've been diagnosed with advanced lung cancer, possibly secondary to the melanoma they removed five years ago.'

Tony took the phone. 'Now listen here, Dad. No-one's going to upstage me! You just hang in there and get yourself some chemotherapy. That's what's keeping me alive.'

But Keith would accept neither surgery nor chemo. He believed that the extra time it might allow him wasn't worth the side effects, so he discharged himself from hospital and went home. During the months that followed he slid downhill fast. Jane and Chris, Lynna and Doug, and Phil and Jenny took turns to visit him most weekends, taking their children along to cheer him up.

Tony, following a philosophical approach to dealing with terminal illness using meditation, reiki and acupuncture, was keen to pass these techniques on to his father and fretted over the fact that Keith was completely disinterested.

When it appeared that Keith had only a short time left, I visited him at his beachside home. We spent a day together, reminiscing about the years we'd shared, the children we'd raised, the houses he'd built, the family holidays he'd survived; we looked through years of photographs, laughing and remembering.

Each of us had a request.

'There's no-one else I can ask to do this,' Keith confided. 'I want to die at home, not in hospital, and my doctor has agreed to come here and help me. I can't ask Connie because she'd prefer me to be in hospital, even now. I'll give you my doctor's name, so you can contact him when the time comes.'

I squeezed his arm. 'I'll do that for you Keith, I promise. And there's something I'd like to suggest that could be quite meaningful for you and Tony.'

He brushed aside the tear welling in his eye.

'Please spend some time with him soon. I know how much he'd appreciate it because he's told me that he'd like to share with you some of the things he's finding helpful, like meditation and reiki. Keith, please let him.'

'Yes, I guess you're right. It would be nice for us to get together, just Tony and me, seeing we're heading in the same direction. How about Tuesday? That's only three days off. Do you think he could make it then?'

Keith called Connie and together we planned the day. Tony and I would arrive at ten, after the community nurse had finished Keith's morning routine. Connie and I would go for a beach walk then have a long lunch at the nearby RSL club, allowing Keith and Tony to while away the day together. Tony was ecstatic, keen for Tuesday morning to arrive.

The opportunity never eventuated. Early on Monday morning, an anxious Lynna was at my door to tell me that Connie had phoned to say she was sending Keith to hospital.

'Mum, he doesn't want to go to hospital. What can we do?' Lynna was frantic.

'We can call his doctor,' I said. 'But it's better if you do the talking. I'll just help you with what to say.'

The doctor arrived that morning and gave him pain relief and an injection to ease his distressed breathing. Relaxed and free from pain, Keith died in the early hours of Tuesday.

Tony was heartbroken. Keith and he had missed their chance to say goodbye. Tony was left hurting, lamenting his lost last opportunity to spend time with his father.

I was saddened and extremely disappointed when I learned a few months later that Keith had made a new will, one that favoured Connie's children and did not include Jane, Phil, Lynna or Tony.

Tony Carden and Bruce Brown, Darlinghurst, 1994.
Photo Courtesy of Jamie Dunbar

HIV risk in line of duty

A police officer faces an agonizing three-month wait to find out whether he has contracted HIV or Hepatitis C after he was allegedly stabbed with a syringe by a suspect.

The Mount Druitt constable is one of hundreds of police, prison and ambulance officers who have undertaken tests for HIV and other transmittable diseases as a result of being stabbed, bitten or exposed to bodily fluids while carrying out their duties.

A personal protection kit containing gloves, disposable masks and waterproof Band-Aids is being distributed to all police officers.

The Sydney Morning Herald, 25 June 1994

Chapter 22

'Only a Pinprick'

> It is a very rare occasion for me to attend a funeral. There have been so many and I feel terrible for not attending but I know what will happen and it bothers me. They end up being impersonal and quickly arranged by those left behind to bury the cadavers. The gay community is reinventing this occasion.
>
> Tony's journal, 1995

1994

In 1990 Tony had trained at ACON to become an AIDS support group facilitator. He'd meet with groups of people newly diagnosed with HIV for a few hours every Wednesday night to help them adjust to their changed lifestyles. He also joined the Positive Speakers Bureau, a program to supply concerned groups with the opportunity to hear firsthand about HIV/AIDS. By 1994 his training as a speaker was taking him to unexpected places in the community, such as dental surgeries to talk with dentists worried about treating HIV/AIDS patients and secondary schools throughout Sydney to hammer home the 'safe sex' message. He'd get the attention of students by holding up a large jar of pills in his left hand.

'Every day for the rest of my life I have to swallow these pills, all twenty-two of them,' he'd tell the awed students holding the pill jar high and rattling it, 'because if I don't, I'll die of AIDS.'

With all eyes focussed on the pills, he'd place them on the desk, pick up a condom, raise it high in his other hand and wave it around. 'AIDS is preventable. I could have avoided my illness if only I'd used one of these!'

Their laughter was probably a ruse to disguise teenage embarrassment, but Tony's message always got through. Letters of appreciation from grateful students frequently arrived at ACON, acknowledging that his candid, confronting approach to an otherwise controversial issue was saving young people's lives, which only encouraged him to continue his work. Claude recalled, 'Over four years Tony spoke to thousands of young people all over Sydney.' It was only with ACON's ongoing support that he was able to keep up this amazing pace. ACON supplied vouchers for the door-to-door taxis that took him to places near and far, wherever his services were required.

Perhaps it was this hectic pace that suggested to the St Vincent's AIDS research team that he'd be an ideal subject for a heart biopsy, to further their understanding of how AIDS affected the heart muscle. Tony willingly obliged, seeing it as a contribution towards conquering the disease.

'It was eerie,' he told me afterwards, 'knowing that the needle was going between my ribs and straight into my heart.'

His compensation was being told that despite AIDS having enlarged his heart, it was very strong and probably wouldn't give up easily.

* * *

'There's going to be an exhibition of AIDS art at the end of the year, at the National Gallery in Canberra,' Tony told me in February, 'and I've decided to do something for it. I'm not an artist and I'm not a crash-hot photographer, either, but I'll think of something.'

For a few weeks he mulled over what form his artwork might take and an idea began to evolve. 'I had the inspiration that this exhibition would be a good opportunity to document AIDS,' he later told an interviewer. 'The work is a representation of people who I believe to be "AIDS warriors" – people who are fighting the AIDS epidemic. I've taken care to make sure that I have a complete cross-section of society on the canvas. There are Catholic nuns, drag queens, actors, politicians, medical professionals . . .'

After his Thursday massage and acupuncture sessions at the neighbourhood centre, he'd stay for the art therapy class and chat with its volunteer teacher, Libby Woodhams. He bounced his concept for his artwork off Libby, who was immediately enthusiastic and offered suggestions to get him started. Libby helped him assemble a toolkit: a large envelope containing business-card-size pieces of heavy art paper, pens, a packet of stainless-steel sewing needles, matches and alcohol.

Over the next few months he sought out 'warriors' in order to collect contributions. Will Conyers, a friend since school days, who had used his roles as a theatrical producer and musical director to provide entertainment and employment for people with AIDS, later described the occasion.

It was a beautiful sunny afternoon when I went to visit Tony in his house at Woolloomooloo. He invited me in, and I sat down. I'd woken him and he was rather drowsy. Tony looked animated as he looked across at me.

'I need your blood, Will.'

'I beg your pardon?' I wondered whether he was still half asleep.

'I just need to get some blood from you. It's for a project I'm doing. I only need a drop of it.'

'What are you talking about, Tony?' I found the notion of thinking about blood in the presence of someone with HIV genuinely scary. He told me about his *Warrior Blood* collage and that he was preparing it for the 'Don't Leave Me This Way – Art in the Age of AIDS' exhibition to be held at the National Gallery in Canberra in November, two months later. He produced an envelope, opened it and showed me a number of squares of thick white paper.

'Take one, Will. It's for your drop of blood.'

Tony took a needle from a pack and waved it over the flame of his gas stove to sterilise it as he said, 'It'll only be a pinprick, Will.'

'I'd be honoured, Tony.'

I took a deep breath and looked at my friend. Yes, that was Tony! You never knew what to expect next. He pricked my thumb and squeezed out a drop of blood. I pressed my thumb on to the square of paper and we both blew together on the blood-stained paper. When it was dry I signed the card.

'I've used their blood,' Tony said of his 'warriors', 'because having your blood on a canvas is pretty powerful, and the work they're doing is very powerful. Using blood is also a little shocking and I like to shock people.'

After four months of similar encounters with over fifty 'warriors', Tony attached the cards to a canvas and signed it. He titled it *Warrior Blood* – work in progress. Then with Libby's help, he framed and glazed it.

'It's finished,' he announced one afternoon, proudly allowing me a sneak preview. 'I've purposely left some of the canvas blank in order to present *Warrior Blood*'s most important message: "Will there be more warriors after I'm gone?" It's a challenge for others to come forward because the battle can't stop yet. There's still more to be done.'

A few days later, *Warrior Blood* was on its way to Canberra, safely in the hands of a National Gallery courier.

* * *

On a crisp Canberra evening I proudly joined a throng of guests for the formal opening of the exhibition. The wide walkway between the High Court and the National Gallery had been transformed into a marquee, its walls and ceilings softly draped in white nylon, and with cream carnations and greenery tucked amongst the folds. Tables lining its sides bore platters of finger-food. To spot Tony, who I knew was here somewhere among the groups of guests milling about sipping champagne and chatting, would be a matter of luck, there were so many people in attendance. *What an eclectic group*, I thought. The gay community was well represented, as were families, businesspeople, health workers, even several politicians.

'I don't know how you Australians manage to pull off something as amazing as this,' a tall, slightly greying, artily dressed American man remarked to me. 'We sure couldn't get away with it in the US. Our government wouldn't give us a cent for anything to do with AIDS.'

'Well, my son has had something to do with it,' I proudly replied. 'In fact, we have laws against discrimination towards homosexuals and people with AIDS here now, thanks to activists like him and some of our politicians,' I replied, introducing myself.

'Pleased to meet you, ma'am,' he said, offering his hand. 'I'm the Director of the Art Institute of Chicago. It makes me sad to think that we can't hold something like this at our gallery, but there's no likelihood of us following Australia's lead with anything even remotely related to homosexuality, let alone AIDS.'

'It is now my pleasure to declare this exhibition open,' announced the speaker who'd welcomed guests and described the lead-up to the exhibition. 'I invite you all into the gallery.'

A falling petal could have shattered the silence, as for a few moments the gathering froze, as though fearing what they might behold in the exhibition. Then slowly, a few at a time, a respectful procession entered the gallery. Beside the door stood a statue, bandaged from head to feet, a dripline emerging through swathes of bandages, silent and still. Then it moved, reaching out its hand. Onlookers gasped, brushing tears from their eyes as they drifted by to the other exhibits. On the gallery's soaring back wall was the Australian Memorial Quilt, made from hundreds of panels, each one sewn by grieving hands. Some works were confronting, others heartrending: photographs, posters, paintings, all expressions of the extent and hopelessness of HIV/AIDS.

AIDS Memorial Quilt unfolding ceremony,
Darling Harbour, 1997.

Facing the end of the walkway to the lower-level gallery hung *Warrior Blood*, visible to all as they descended the ramp. It was surrounded by an animated crowd of viewers.

After Tony died, I found among his books a small volume by Ted Gott, the exhibition's curator, titled *Don't Leave Me This Way*. Inside the front page was a pink ribbon sealed with a red heart so I knew Tony had meant it for me. In a very frail hand he'd written:

'Only a Pinprick'

February 19 1995

Lesley,

This was presented to me for my work and involvement in the exhibition in Canberra. It has been a phenomenal success, ten thousand visitors a week.

You take care of this, and when it's time please hand it on in the family.

With pride,
Tony-oni-Macaroni

P.S. The curator has told me that my piece, *Warrior Blood*, enjoyed the most attention and interest. Who would have dreamed?'

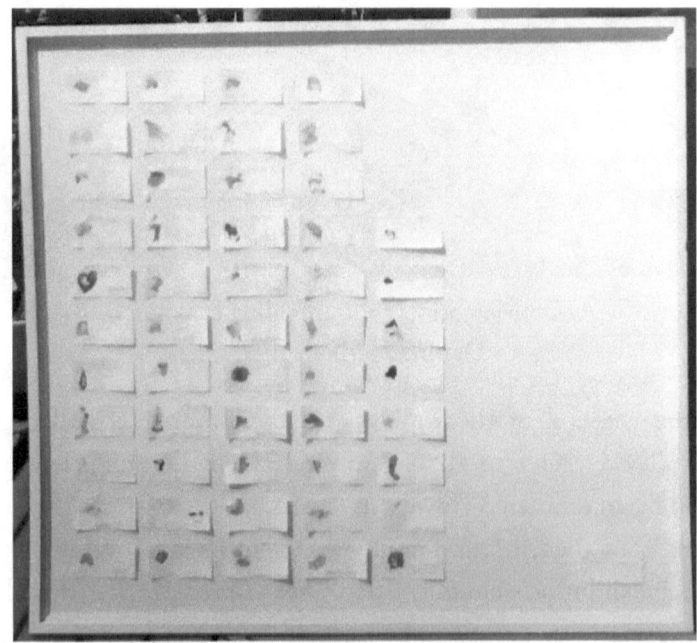

Tony's *Warrior Blood*, featured in *Campaign* magazine, 2014.

The red ribbon is the universal symbol of awareness and support for people living with HIV. Wearing a red ribbon is a great way to raise awareness on and during the run up to World AIDS Day.

In 1991 in New York's East Village a group of artists came up with what would become one of the most recognized symbols of the decade: the Red Ribbon.

It has been seen in such high-profile places as the red carpet of the Oscars, and the Freddie Mercury Tribute Concert at London's Wembley Stadium in 1992 where over 100,000 were distributed among the audience.

www.worldaidsday.org

Chapter 23

The Orange Branch

> Last year I lost my granny, my daddy, 350 T-cells, my meticulous approach to pill-popping, and so many friends I can no longer stop to mourn.
>
> There was a day long ago when I did not think of AIDS. Now it is my nemesis, dragging from a heavy chain. Oh, please let it end.
>
> Tony's journal, 1995

As our family sat toasting Christmas 1994, a taxi pulled up outside and into the sunshine sprang Tony, a glowing smile enhancing his yellow patterned waistcoat and amber beads.

'Merry Christmas, everyone. Ho, ho, ho. There are presents in my bag here for each of you and don't go fretting about me overspending, because I haven't. They're all from the two-dollar shop and so are the paper and cards.'

The white pottery cherub he gave me that day still sits on my dressing table among the withered rose petals in a basket of potpourri that belonged to Tony.

Tony entertained us non-stop over lunch, his spirits so lively I wondered what he'd taken. After little fingers had extracted the last silver coin from the Christmas pudding, he placed a brightly illustrated booklet on the table. It was titled: 'Uncle Max Has AIDS'.

Tony had personalised it by inserting the nickname favoured by his nieces and nephews.

'I'd like to read this to the children, as a way of preparing them,' he proposed.

'No, Tony. No!' came the chorus from Phil, Lynna and Jane. 'Definitely not on Christmas Day.'

His face slumped and the matter was dropped.

* * *

1995

For some time the Crystal House's steep, narrow staircase had posed a problem for Tony. Despondent about no longer being able to enjoy soaking in the upstairs bathtub, which he found so restorative, he reluctantly asked Clover for help. That was how a small flat in a high-rise block in Pelican Street, off Oxford Street, complete with bathtub, became his new home.

On a sultry February morning, volunteers from the Bobby Goldsmith Foundation blew in like a fresh autumn breeze, packed his possessions, loaded their truck and moved Tony to his new address. They even provided him with a second-hand refrigerator, microwave and vacuum cleaner. He was sad to leave the Crystal House, but with Biche by his side, an outdoor armchair and a few potted plants on the north-facing balcony, he was resigned to adapting to his new home.

Every Tuesday he visited St Vincent's AIDS clinic to join others with advanced KS[21] for chemotherapy. They'd spend several hours seated in armchairs, feet up, arms attached to drips, while their bodies took in the toxic infusions. Self-pity could easily have prevailed, but instead the Tuesday clinic had become a place of bawdy merriment ever since Tony had begun filling the room with roars of laughter, from the

---

21 Kaposi sarcoma.

nurses to the patients, with his far-fetched stories about Oxford Street exploits. They laughed even knowing that later in the day nausea and diarrhoea would overtake them, and the next time they shampooed or brushed their hair, tufts would gather in the shower or hairbrush until eventually little would remain.

Tony told me only as much as he thought I could handle, but not enough to draw me too deeply into his suffering. Most details of his illness he kept private. Even so, aware of how miserable chemo could make people feel, every Tuesday I'd either wait outside his apartment ready to greet him when he stepped out of Tiffany's Transport bus or visit him later in the afternoon and stay just long enough to have a cup of tea and to replenish his pantry cupboard. All he wanted was to get into bed and sleep it off, and all I wanted was peace of mind in knowing he was okay.

One Tuesday I waited and waited but no Tiffany's Transport arrived. Eventually I took the lift to his second-floor apartment and knocked on the door, thinking he may have returned early. There was no response. I tried calling through the keyhole, but still nothing, so I dumped my box of groceries, sat down on the stairs and waited, cursing the fact that he refused to give a spare key to anyone, not even one of his friends, so ferociously did he guard his independence. I phoned Phil, who arrived later in the afternoon. We discussed our options and decided to call the police. Two sprightly 'boys in blue' sprinted up the stairs and listened as we gave them a brief outline of Tony's situation and why we were concerned.

'Stand back while I force the door open,' the burlier of the two warned. 'We'll go in first because we don't know what we might find.'

I held my breath. The apartment was orderly, but empty. *Where was he?* Phil and I, remembering the previous time he'd gone missing, considered ourselves old hands at dealing with his disappearances. We tracked down his Community Support Network carers Andrew and Tracey. Andrew was worried but could shed no light, leaving Tracey, whose answering machine informed us she'd be away for the next four days in her role as a Qantas flight attendant.

We called Qantas and explained our predicament to an admin officer, who assured us she would get a message to Tracey when her plane reached its destination. Three hours later, Tracey called to relate the whole debacle: Tony had called her early that morning. 'Does Qantas have a flight to New Zealand today and if so, could you arrange a ticket for me?' he'd asked.

'Sure, Tony,' Tracey had replied. 'The answer to both is yes, but you'll have just over an hour to get to the airport. Can you manage that?'

He'd assured her he'd be there and asked her to contact me later in the morning to let me know where he'd gone. Tracey had agreed, but that's where his plan had fallen apart. Tracey had left the request with office staff, who'd somehow failed to carry it out.

Tony, upset by the trouble he'd caused, later explained. 'I woke up on Tuesday morning and the thought of chemotherapy gave me the horrors. I just couldn't do it. They paid me the previous week for the work I did for the anti-discrimination campaign so I thought, *Bugger it! I'm off to New Zealand to visit Bronte.* She worked with me on the campaign and had often invited me to come over and celebrate its success, but I could never afford to go. I did ask Tracey to let you know but somehow the wires must have got crossed. I'm so sorry, Lezzles.'

* * *

It was now five years since Tony's diagnosis, but such vitality emanated from his battered body, I couldn't believe he would die. Death wouldn't dare take him!

The excitement in his voice when he phoned early in the New Year radiated optimism.

'There's a new GP in the area and I visited her recently because I'd heard she has been helping people with their AIDS medications. She'd like to talk to you, Lezzles. It's about a new AIDS medication she thinks could be a breakthrough.'

Penny,[22] originally a physiotherapist, was motivated by a determination to make a significant contribution to the AIDS battle and had returned to university to study medicine. Her down-to-earth approach to the reality of his illness gave him confidence. He felt fortunate to have found her.

When we were beckoned into her surgery I immediately warmed to her enthusiastic manner.

'Tony's told me you have a background in pathology so I'd like to discuss with you a new medication that I think could stop the AIDS virus in its tracks.'

She drew a diagram of the virus's method of attack and the vital role that an enzyme called protease plays in its replication.

'This new medication is called a "protease inhibitor" because that's what it does – it interferes with the virus's protease connection, and without that the virus can't multiply.'

The simple logic behind the new drug was easy to understand. It saddened me that its discovery had taken so long, that solutions to AIDS were so like needles in haystacks.

'But there's a problem,' Penny confessed. 'The medication isn't available yet and it won't be for some time. I can get hold of a small experimental supply from America, but it wouldn't be cheap, and you'd have to pay for it.'

Tony's eyes shone with hope.

'If it might help, let's try it,' I agreed.

A look of relief spread across Tony's face.

Penny suggested that protease inhibitors would probably work best

---

22 Pseudonym.

in the absence of other drugs, so Tony discontinued ddC, ddI and AZT and took the plunge with the new medication alone.

Professor Cooper, from St Vincent's Hospital, was adamant. 'No, Tony. You mustn't stop your medications. Those anti-viral drugs are what's keeping you alive.'

But Tony had made his decision. He'd take the one-drug gamble.

* * *

'Put the shopping down and come with me to St Vincent's. I have something to show you.'

I'd called into the Oxford Street corner store for few groceries before joining Tony for a chat and a cup of tea. He seemed sprightlier than usual, and as we walked to the car to drive the short distance we'd once have walked his eagerness sparked my curiosity. Past the main entrance he led me, and in through the hospital's former sandstone entry. I realised we were heading for Ward 17 South and felt apprehensive, remembering my first visit there. As the lift doors opened, he grinned and ushered me out. I stopped, amazed. Gone were the open, doorless wards, the rows of beds, the air of grim despair. Pastel-coloured walls now boasted colourful artworks and a carpeted room invited visitors to relax in lounge chairs and enjoy a coffee while they waited.

'Quite a change, isn't it? Come on down the hall and I'll show you the rest,' he urged. 'It's totally transformed.'

In place of the open, multi-bed wards were a series of single and two-bed rooms with curtains and blinds at the windows, which, very importantly, gave the patients privacy and a new feeling of dignity. I was impressed. The doctors' and nurses' station was open and inviting, located so as to ensure visitors were attended to properly.

'Now for the highlight,' Tony announced, opening with a flourish a door labelled 'Bathroom'.

'Tra-la! Here's what's been the biggest challenge of all.'

The room was spacious and bright. The newly tiled floor and walls gleamed, and across the far wall a row of shower recesses with stools and hand-held showerheads awaited their first occupants. Taking up almost half the area was a wide, deep bathtub with access steps and an overhead hoist.

'This bathtub took some bargaining, I can tell you. It came from the US and it cost a mint, but believe me, it'll be worth every dollar. The side opens so really sick patients can just slide in and out. And look – hydrotherapy water jets and a backrest so you can enjoy a good soak – something that really makes a difference to an aching body. I know from experience.'

His pride in his achievement and his determination that his fellow AIDS travellers would feel cossetted, not rejected, touched me. I was aware that he and Clover had lobbied over a long period of time for government funding to upgrade the AIDS ward.

'The extra luxury is all thanks to an older man who died of AIDS last year and left us a pretty sizable legacy,' Tony continued. 'Along with what the government provided, it meant we could turn this into a home away from home for AIDS patients. They deserve it – they go through so much.'

'Congratulations, Tony! It's a world away from that chamber of horrors that used to be Seventeen South.' I hugged him, feeling bones no longer padded by muscle, wondering what challenge he'd apply himself to next.

* * *

Many young men with AIDS, having lost faith in the cure that lingered around the corner but never arrived, had cashed in their superannuation and blown it on one last bucket-list grand trip. One young man, who'd pleaded with his partner to 'take me to Paris, Johnny' and his partner's subsequent story of that last trip, must have set Tony thinking. He had no superannuation, but he did have a brand-new

Lesley and Tony in Darlinghurst, 1995.
Photo courtesy of Jamie Dunbar

bank account with ten thousand dollars in it, which John Marsden, a lawyer active in the area of equal rights for the gay community, had won for him following a successful challenge to Keith's will.

Tony wasn't without a bucket list of his own: *Angels in America*, a show he'd longed to see, was staging on Broadway in June, as were *Hello, Dolly* and *Les Miserables*. New York City beckoned. He'd blow his winnings on one last visit and, thanks to Keith, he'd do it in style.

When Tracey arrived the following afternoon, he asked her to arrange a first-class return ticket to New York for the following Friday. Next, he called his Manhattan friend Kurt, who agreed to book a single ensuite room at the Waldorf Astoria for the weekend. Tony began to pack.

It was three days of no-holds-barred fun with friends and three nights of Broadway's best in the city he'd called home. How he managed it all in his frail state still staggers me, but his determination and aplomb somehow enabled him to pull it off.

He was back before we'd noticed his absence. It was only years later that I was able to join the dots about his final fling.

* * *

My mother, Mary, died in 1994, and with the money she left me I bought a cottage at Hawks Nest, near Newcastle, and sometimes took Tony there for a break. Late in the day we'd drive to Myall Lake to sit by the shore and watch the orange sun sink into the lake, its black swans silhouetted against the skyline, while we nibbled on snacks and sipped wine.

'When the time comes,' he told me one afternoon, 'I'd like my life to end somewhere beautiful like this – where I can hear the surf and watch the black swans at sunset.'

Tony and I agreed on a plan. When he felt the time was right, we'd move together to the Hawks Nest cottage, where I would care for him during his final days. I contacted the AIDS ward at Newcastle's John Hunter Hospital, and they agreed to arrange for the district nurse and the AIDS nursing support team to visit us three times every week to support us. It would be a stressful time, I knew, but it was the pressure it would place on our relationship that concerned me most. Tony could be a difficult taskmaster. I realised that we were nearing the next, final stage of his life and that his gamble of relying on just one medication was not paying off.

During recent visits to his apartment, I'd noticed he was sleeping more and I'd had to knock and call out several times before he stumbled out of bed to answer the door. His need for warmth made the apartment so stuffy it was difficult to breathe, so I'd been wondering how Andrew, Tracey and the rest of his team of carers were coping. Not unexpectedly, Susan, Tony's social worker from community health, called me one afternoon. 'I've decided to arrange a meeting to work out a plan of action for Tony's carers. The occupational therapist and the community nurse will be there too so they can have some input as well. Tony needs around-the-clock care now, as you're probably aware, but he's determined to stay at home as long as he can.'

When I arrived, a discussion circle had been formed, with Tony, looking relaxed in his green chair, enjoying a coffee and chatting with his carer Andrew, and Alison, the community nurse. He beamed a warm smile at me as I took a chair. Susan listed the items for discussion and Andrew added a couple more. The occupational therapist, who'd inspected the flat, suggested that safety-rails be installed and the bathroom modified, and the community nurse agreed to come by every morning to assist with bathing and medications. Then Susan drew up a twenty-four-hour, seven-day care roster and prepared a contact list for everyone.

When she asked whether there were any other concerns for Tony's wellbeing, feeling like a traitor, I raised my hand.

'I think someone should have a key to Tony's apartment,' I ventured, avoiding his eyes. 'Sometimes it's difficult for him to get to the door and if he's too ill, or if he takes a tumble, we should have access to a spare key.'

'I don't want anyone to have a key to my apartment except me,' Tony said firmly. 'I've managed until now and I still can.'

But Susan, his social worker, was adamant. His face fell as he dug into his pocket and reluctantly handed over his key. 'Here, get one cut.'

That afternoon he relinquished not only his key but also what he treasured most: his independence.

* * *

One morning the following week his longstanding GP, Dr Marilyn McMurchie, rang and invited me to visit her. The patients sitting around her waiting room were all young men, some bright and cheerful-looking, others lean and pale, one with ominous purple lesions blushing through a thin veil of make-up. It hurt to see them, so young, their lank bodies and sunken eyes betraying their common scourge. One by one they disappeared into the surgery then re-emerged looking hopeful, clutching a bundle of prescriptions as they left to go to the pharmacy. As the last one left, the doctor beckoned me from her surgery door.

'Please come in, Lesley.'

She drew a folded sheet of blue paper from an envelope.

'Tony left this poem with me. He wanted me to understand how he feels about his illness, and I think it may help you to understand, too. He puts on a brave face most of the time, because that's Tony. But this poem reveals what's really going on in his mind, so I'd like to share it with you.'

Written on the blue paper in Tony's wavering handwriting was a Tennessee Williams poem from *The Night of the Iguana*. Our eyes met as we both blinked back tears.

At last Tony had found a way to share with us his anguish of living with AIDS:

> How calmly does the orange branch
> Observe the sky begin to blanch
> Without a cry, without a prayer
> With no betrayal of despair.
>
> Some time while night obscures the tree
> The zenith of its life will be
> Gone past forever,
> And from thence
> A second history will commence.

A chronicle no longer old,
A bargaining with mist and mould,
And finally, the broken stem
The plummeting to earth; and then

An intercourse not well designed
For beings of a golden kind
Whose native green must arch above
The earth's obscene, corrupting love.

And still the ripe fruit and the branch
Observe the sky begin to blanch
Without a cry, without a prayer
With no betrayal of despair.

Oh, courage could you not as well
Select a second place to dwell,
Not only in that golden tree
But in the frightened heart of me?

I read and re-read the poem until it became etched into my mind, where it will remain forever. The orange tree's message of its 'frightened heart' tore at me – Tony had always been so positive, so certain he'd survive, and his infectious optimism had made me certain too. Now, through the words of a poem, he'd revealed what he'd kept hidden – his fear.

June 1995 – In the US the FDA approve compassionate and research access to saquinavir, the first in a new class of drugs called 'Protease Inhibitors' which is said to be some of the most helpful news in years for people living with AIDS.

The Albion Centre, *A HIV/AIDS Timeline*

Chapter 24

Freesias

I think it is important to concentrate on the wonderful things that have happened. My life has probably been fuller than ninety-nine per cent of people on the planet. I've done nearly everything I wanted to do and more, and achieved many dreams. I die feeling accomplished and I think that is the most important thing.

There are a few people who have been through hell over the last few years at my expense – that's my family: my brother Philip; Jane and Carolyn, my sisters; and my mother and my grandmother. They've been put through a lot and I want them to know that my appreciation may not always have seemed to have been there, but it was, it was just very difficult sometimes.

Tony's farewell video, July 1995

August 1995

Embracing death at 33, an age when it was the norm to be embracing life was the conflict at the core of every AIDS diagnosis. So AIDS sufferers devised a way to empower themselves during the last weeks of their journey. With little else to look forward to, they planned their own funerals. Tony had told me nothing about his plan, only that when the time came I should visit the Reverend Erica Mathieson at St James Church, opposite the Supreme Court of New South Wales in downtown Sydney.

'It'll all come together, Lezzles, I promise you. There's no need to worry, I've arranged everything.'

Instead, he drew my attention to his final resting place, Waverley Cemetery, overlooking the ocean, where he knew many of our ancestors rested.

We met there one windy afternoon to wander through the maze of narrow, overgrown paths, headstone-spotting as though we were admiring old masters at the Louvre. Australian poets Henry Lawson, Dorothea Mackellar and Henry Kendall are buried there, but it was American actor William E Sheridan who clinched it for Tony. He assured me lightly that although he'd have preferred Bette Davis, William would be amenable company. We located the family plot and he asked for a photograph, cheekily laughing and waving at the camera from behind the greying marble centrepiece of his grave-to-be, a youthful flying angel.

'By the way, I'd like the White Ladies to be my undertakers, because I don't want any men handling my body. And, if it's okay with you, I'd like a white coffin as well.'

He was keeping the conversation light – with so much heartache hovering over us it seemed pointless to do otherwise. Picking up on his mood, I ignored the macabre undertones and tried to match his cheerful banter, sensing that his greatest sadness lay in knowing the pain his death would bring to us, his family.

Within days of our visit, the community nurse took Tony to St Vincent's, where he was admitted into Ward 17 South. Despite the hope offered by the protease inhibitor, and regardless of his positivity, the malign lesions of Kaposi sarcoma had spread ruthlessly throughout his body – the gamble of relying on the single medication had not paid off. The nurse also convinced me that to take him to Hawks Nest would be a very stressful exercise for us both. Never again would he enjoy the black swans on the lake at sunset.

* * *

Tony's last birthday celebration, Centennial Park, December, 1994.
Standing: Elizabeth Morson with friend Rodney Jones.
Seated from right: Lesley, Jane, Tony, nephew Matthew, niece Phoebe,
Lynna with baby Natalie, Ben, sister-in-law Jenny Carden with baby Sam.
From left: nephew Daniel, nephew Jamie.
Photograph Courtesy of C. Moore Hardy

In a peaceful room at the end of the corridor overlooking Paddington's narrow terraced streets lay Tony, an intravenous tube gently dripping a soothing potion into his arm.

'Hi, Lezzles,' he smiled, without sitting up. 'I thought it was time I tried Seventeen South's new face lift.'

I arranged some peaches and grapes in a bowl and drew up a chair.

'If you look down there at the second row of terraces you can see Hugo's house. It's the third from the left, the one with the green roof.'

So began the final stretch of his remarkable journey, a month-long vigil that would see me clamber up the chasm's highest slopes to experience at last, bruised and battered, the radiance of his 'other family'.

During the first week of his hospital stay I visited every day, morning or afternoon, retreating to the waiting room whenever doctors, nurses or visitors appeared. Dr Cole,[23] the ward Registrar, would catch my eye as I passed the nurses' station and update me on Tony's condition and treatment. Despite his frailty, Tony loved visitors and enjoyed holding court when several arrived at the same time.

By the second week, he was bright in the mornings but during the afternoons he often drifted away, even in mid-conversation. *It's time*, I thought:

'I think you should have this letter, Dr Cole. It's from Tony and it explains his end-of-life wishes.'

Dr Cole looked concerned as he took Tony's document and read it. 'What he's asking for is perfectly clear, Mrs Saddington, and we'll do our best to follow it. However as far as the drip's concerned, it is life-extending, but on the other hand, without it he'd suffer even more because of dehydration, so that's a decision only you can make. We'll cease his medications tomorrow and start him on some morphine.'

Although I queried it, we continued the drip.

Most mornings, Clover called in on her way to her office, bringing freesias each day until the room was filled with their heady fragrance.

'They're Tony's favourite flowers,' she told me.

The following morning, when Tony was very lucid, Dr Cole drew up a chair beside his bed.

'Tony, I've read your letter and we'll do everything we can to follow your wishes. That means that tomorrow we'll be stopping the Bactrim and the protease inhibitors.'

'But I don't want to die,' exclaimed a confused and distraught Tony, shaking his head. 'And I don't want to start on morphine too early, either, because I don't want my body to get used to it. That way, when the pain gets really bad, I'll get the best value out of it.'

The agony of this moment overwhelmed me. I wondered whether

---

23 Pseudonym.

handing over his letter had only worsened his ordeal. Dr Cole's anguish was clear as his eyes met mine.

Professor Cooper also dropped by most mornings.

'I suppose you'll be sending me to the hospice soon?' Tony asked him one day.

'No, Tony,' Professor Cooper assured him. 'You can stay here as long as you wish. You deserve that, and tomorrow we'll put you onto that wonderful massage mattress you managed to get hold of.'

Another week drifted by, with Tony drifting too, in and out of consciousness.

'Would you like us to put a sofa-chair in Tony's room? That way you can stay here. It would probably make it easier for you both.'

'Thanks, but I don't think having his mother sleeping in his room would work for Tony.'

'In that case, there's a small sitting room on the other side of the ward. I'll have it made up for you.'

Visitors, family and friends, streamed in, stayed awhile, dabbed their eyes and left. A few of his friends I recognised, others not, until gradually we grew familiar and discovered we had much to share.

'Where's he been hiding you?' they'd ask.

'Where's he been hiding *you*?' I'd reply.

Tony's two families had at last found each other.

Hugo and Itty, Tony's friends since schooldays, sat by his bedside softly singing bawdy songs (to nursery rhyme tunes) that they'd sung as teenagers. They believed, as did I, that a patient in a coma could hear and comprehend.

'Isn't that sweet?' remarked a nurse one day. 'His two friends singing nursery rhymes to him. They've probably known each other since childhood.'

I smirked, grateful that the ward's poor acoustics were muffling the ribald lyrics.

Will, Tony's longstanding friend, musician and AIDS warrior, who'd kept in constant contact since I'd told him of Tony's decline, had flown from Melbourne to share my vigil. We grew close, becoming regulars at a nearby Lebanese restaurant, where we'd drown our sorrows in a few glasses of red wine so I could return to Tony's bedside revitalised as the days dragged by.

Someone called Agnes appeared; her New York accent and rapport with Tony revealing they had history. A trained nurse, Agnes taught me how to massage his bony feet with a Chinese herbal balm, to avoid the hazards of pressure sores. I'd sit by him, playing the music he loved, talking softly, and retreat to the waiting room to allow others their share of private time with him.

At ten o'clock one night his bedside phone rang.

'Hello Lesley, this is Steph Whitmont. How's it going?'

Steph, who'd shared meaningful times with Tony in New York during the eighties, now lived nearby in Paddington.

'Just the same, Steph. He's asleep and I'm sitting here with him.'

'Is there anything you'd like?'

'Nothing, thanks, Steph.'

'Are you sure? If you could have just one thing right now, what would it be?'

'Well, if you'd really like to know I'd kill for a brandy and dry.'

'I'll be there shortly.'

Half an hour later Steph appeared, with brandy, dry ginger ale, champagne, glasses, and temptingly aromatic hot pasta from a nearby Italian trattoria. We sat on either side of Tony's bed, drank brandy and dries, ate pasta, toasted him with champagne and included him as much as we could in our party. Just after midnight Steph crept out. I kissed Tony's forehead and tiptoed across the corridor to bed.

'Mrs Saddington, are you awake?' an unfamiliar voice interrupted my slumber. 'Tony's gone.'

Shattered thoughts gradually coalesced in my mind. It was over and Tony had chosen privacy for his final exit . . .

I sat with him until dawn, determined to linger there beside him until they came to take him away. Until then he still belonged to life.

As dark, silent hours drifted towards a new day, I pondered the things I'd discovered during the past long month: that Tony had replaced his passionate determination during life with a calm dignity in dying; that he'd attended retreats in the Southern Highlands, arranged by Claude, and there had discovered the comforting spirituality that had fortified his final months; that Agnes had been matched with him two years ago to provide special care in handling the hurdles of his health problems and medications; his other family's strength and loyalty . . .

The stars faded and the sky's darkness lifted to reveal drifts of silver-streaked mauve. I called Jane and Will.

* * *

Clover's Obituary for Tony

In his farewell video Tony told us that he had done all the things that he had wanted to do – and with what flair and boldness!

Tony and I started working together in 1991 to get desperately needed funding for Ward 17, the HIV/AIDS ward at St Vincent's Hospital. Tony worked with ACT UP to gain awareness. He was involved in everything from setting up a 'hospital ward' in front of the Health Minister's house to gatecrashing the 1992 National AIDS conference at Darling Harbour to presenting 907 white carnations – representing the number of people who had died of AIDS-related illness in Australia during the year. He even handed out information in Pitt Street on World AIDS Day dressed in a dressing gown and slippers.

Tony and I organised a number of AIDS forums at parliament where we brought together groups to develop dialogue. I was always pleased when I was addressing public meetings and rallies to look down and see Tony in the crowd because he always led the cheering and booing – he was a great public activist.

While he could be demanding and outrageous, he was the most supportive and appreciative person, whether it be for the staff on Ward 17, immunologist Professor David Cooper, Sister Margaret Mines, his carers, or Carole Ann King, who runs the Luncheon Club.

Tony wanted us to remember his contribution to the fight against AIDS and he wanted us to hand on the baton. It is tragic to think of the loss of such a young talented life.

As journalist Michael Glynn wrote of Tony, 'A shining star has fallen from our sky.'

> Clover Moore, Obituaries, *The Australian*, 20 October 1995

PART 4
Requiem

History, despite its wrenching pain,
Cannot be unlived, and if faced
With courage, need not be lived again
    'On the pulse of morning', Maya Angelou, American poet,
              memoirist and civil rights activist, 1993

When I pass away from this earth there are specific things that are important to me. I love churches but have little time for most of the occupants – too much hypocrisy, too many contradictions. Presently I am organising not a traditional funeral but instead a celebration of my very full life.

As a veteran performer I seek the grandeur a funeral can command. I see endless opportunities to express feelings of excruciating loss, of the freedom death brings.

It's my attempt to demystify death.

What an incredible life I have had, peppered with humour and irony; so many good times . . .

The location is important for the peace and charm of a historic old church. My casket will be present throughout the ceremony, in centre place; the end of a treasured life and the folly of life's brevity.

My spiritual beliefs I have protected in a private corner of my being. Spirituality doesn't need constant rambling and raving to exist, only truth, love and dignity.

I want to leave as exquisite a memory for my loved ones as I can impart, using the wonderful talents and communication of my friends to convey the power of love through words, music and poetry.

Tony's journal, 1995

Lynna with daughter Natalie sewing Tony's panel for the Memorial Quilt, Centennial Park, 1996.

Tony's quilt panel – 'Max' was a family nickname, 1997.

Chapter 25

Final Bow

> Please celebrate my life. Don't mourn it. I do not feel robbed, nor do I feel that it is a tragedy that my life has ended at an early age. I have done more than most people would ever dream of and it has been wonderful.
>
> Tony's farewell video, September 1995

September 1995

The numbness I'd felt since Tony died sent me into automatic-pilot mode. With much to be done, I knew my main challenge would be to unearth his plan and somehow to bring it to fruition. I visited St James Church as instructed to meet the Reverend Erica Mathieson. Tony's prediction that it would all come together was spot on.

'My priestess Erica Mathieson is a strong woman who approaches her task with an incredible air of assurance and control, listening always. I could not be more pleased that we are working on this service together. When she refers to "Tony", I want her to know of whom she speaks.'

When I arrived at the plain 1830s convict-era church, the white-cassocked Erica was expecting me. She invited me into the vestry where she revealed what they'd planned. And gradually, over the ensuing days I discovered the extent to which Tony had choreographed his service. The cast was impressive.

'Lesley, I thought I'd better let you know,' said his long-time friend Hugo, 'Tony asked me to read a poem. It's from Tennessee Williams' *The Night of the Iguana* and I promised him I would.'

Lyle would play the stately church organ; Clover Moore, schoolfriend Simon Hunt and Phil were to present eulogies; Will Conyers would fly from Melbourne to sing 'The Impossible Dream' from *Les Miserables*; opera singer Joan Carden was to deliver the aria 'Dido's Lament' from Henry Purcell's opera *Dido and Aeneas* in her rich soprano voice: 'When I am laid, am laid in earth to rest . . . Remember me . . . but ah, forget my fate . . .' Erica would officiate and lead us all in the singing of Tony's chosen hymn: 'He who would valiant be, 'gainst all disaster,' an appropriate choice for a warrior. Every member of the cast knew their role but none had seen the full script.

Only one wish was declined: Tony had requested that the congregation leave the church to the strains of 'Put on your Sunday clothes, there's lots of world out there' from *Hello, Dolly!* but for the Reverend Erica it wasn't reverent enough, so we played it at the graveside instead as thirty-three balloons floated skywards and drifted over Oxford Street before floating up to join Tony's spirit somewhere in the endless blue.

I realised his memorial service was his departing gift to us all. Hopefully, he'd have approved of the extra touches I added. He'd told his nephews and nieces he'd be leaving one day soon so they assumed, having no idea where he planned to go, that when he did, they'd be part of the celebration he'd told them about. They loved him so, having each excelled in his 'how to be naughty' and 'how to trick grown-ups' lessons. So when the day arrived, I organised for them to be given baskets of flowers with which to decorate the pews and strew the aisles.

On a table by the church door, instead of the customary guest book, I spread a rainbow flag and a black marker pen alongside, in anticipation of farewell messages from Tony's friends. They filled the coloured panels with heartfelt missives.

From the moment we entered the church till the last balloon disappeared from sight, the entire service was the grand performance Tony had planned. Was he there? I believe so.

3-Drug Therapy Shows Promise against AIDS

A combination of an experimental anti-AIDS drug and two licensed ones appears to be the most powerful AIDS therapy ever tested on infected patients, a researcher from the experimental drug's developer said at a scientific meeting here today.

The three-drug combination reduced the amount of HIV, the AIDS virus, by 99 percent to levels that could not be detected by standard laboratory tests in 24 of 26 patients.

The two marketed drugs are AZT and 3TC, which the Glaxo Wellcome company makes as Retrovir and Epivir.

The experimental drug is Merck's Indinovir, a member of a new class of anti-AIDS drugs known as Protease Inhibitors.

The New York Times, 30 January 1996

Chapter 26

Return of the Warriors

Tony Carden was a chameleon and shapeshifter to the many people who loved him. He was decadent, hilarious, gaudy, caustic, brilliant and charming. He was often exasperating and exhausting. Tony lived and died a drama queen, an activist, a Clarins addict, and a star.

Kirsty Machon, journalist and fellow activist,
Sydney Star Observer, October 1995

Warrior Blood
List of Warriors

Bates, Julie – Advocate for NSW Sex Workers and for NSW Users and AIDS Association; Awarded Order of Australia Medal in 2018; Principal of Urban Realists Planning and Health Consultants.

Baxter, Don – Executive Director of ACON '80's/'90's; AFAO (Australian Federation of AIDS Organisations); Member of the Order of Australia Medal, 2014; Activist for Gay Rights; 30 years of active involvement in HIV responses in Australia.

Black, Benjamin – Pet groomer and minder for PLWHA; Luncheon Club volunteer; Community Street Patrol; Poverty SUX Campaign.

Blackwood, Agnes – Volunteer Nursing Support group facilitator (trained at Mayo Clinic, US) R.I.P. (2014)

Bredin, Andrew – CSN Support carer, trainer and group facilitator; Phone counsellor for Gay and Lesbian Counselling Service; Facilitator with SMART Recovery (Self-help for drug users and alcoholics).

Brasklin, Jane – Journalist, *Sydney Morning Herald*; publicised gay bashings & poofter-bashing.

Chan, Lyle – Member of ACT UP and spokesperson; ACON treatments officer; imported drugs for Sydney buyers' club; Composer of *An AIDS Activist's Memoir in Music*.

Connolly, Anne – AIDS Pathologist; NSW Health advocate for PLWHA.

Cooper, Professor David – Australia's leading clinical researcher in the field of HIV and related blood-borne viruses; Director of the Kirby Institute; HIV research and treatment and implementation of antiretroviral therapy; Advisor to WHO/UNAIDS; Manager of HIV/AIDS patients at St Vincents Hospital. R.I.P. (2018)

Conyers, Will – Actor, singer, dancer, theatrical director and teacher; Supporter of Melbourne and Sydney HIV/AIDS patients and their families; Director of *STATUS* – Melbourne theatre production about HIV/AIDS for World AIDS Conference in Melbourne, 2014.

Crawford, David – Nursing Unit Client Manager of Ward 17 South; Northern Sydney Area Health Service Clinical Nurse Consultant; Albion Street AIDS International Unit.

Crooks, Levinia – ACON President 1988/'89 and 1991/'92. R.I.P. (2017)

Dart, Frances – Group Account Manager for Burson-Marsteller (contractor to Federal Government to promote the 1993 National AIDS Anti-Discrimination Campaign); Commitment to HIV/AIDS education, particularly discrimination and homophobia.

De Saxe, Mannie – Member of ACT UP; Founder/ Manager of Sydney Park AIDS Memorial Groves (SPAIDS).

Douglas, Grant.

Duffin, Ross – Member of ACT UP and protest facilitator; ACON Education Manager, Committee member and AIDS educator; Journalist.

Dunbar, Jamie – Professional photographer, Photographic record of Sydney's HIV/AIDS epidemic now with Mitchell Library.

Dunne, Stephen – Journalist and Theatre Reviewer, *Sydney Star Observer*.

Fabian, Claude – Member of ACT UP and protest facilitator; Jeweller for LGBTQI+ community for Mardi Gras etc.

Foltyn, Peter – Dental surgeon providing education for dentists treating HIV/AIDS patients.

Foster, Stephen.

Glynn, Michael – Journalist and 1979 Founder of *Sydney Star Observer*; Established Australia's first Gay Business Association; Founder/co-ordinator of the Volunteer Street Patrol; AIDS Poverty Sux Campaign. R.I.P. (1996)

Handley, Ron – Entertainer, provided Cabaret style entertainment as 'Fanny Farquar' of 'Dot and Fanny' with David Wilkins as 'Dot Dingle', at the Newtown Hotel. R.I.P. (1996)

Hardy, C Moore – Professional photographer, specialised in HIV/AIDS photography; *Sydney Morning Herald* photographer; AIDS epidemic Collection now with Mitchell Library.

Hoskins, Mark – Manager, ACON HIV Support Unit, 1993; Management committee PLWHA; ACON Department manager.

Johnson, Lois – Member of ACT UP Canberra, played a significant role in the D-Day protest at Parliament House.

King, Carole Ann – Founder and Manager of The Luncheon Club and The Larder (14 years).

Machon, Kirsty – Member of ACT UP, facilitator of several protests; AIDS medications specialist; Journalist.

McMurchie, Marilyn – Doctor, Darlinghurst Medical Centre.

Maguire, Carolyn – Tony's sister; Featured with Tony and her son Jamie in the Anti-Discrimination Campaign 'Someone's Uncle'.

Malcolm, Anne – Worked at Albion Street Clinic; Head of ACON Community services Unit.

Marshall, Keith – Cognitive Behaviour Therapist and psychologist who worked as Psychologist/Counsellor at ACON.

Mines, Sister Margaret – Catholic nun, Sister of Charity; St Vincent's Pastoral Care Department carer for AIDS patients and their families; Founder of Carinya (Koori word for Home) in the late '80s to provide support for people living with HIV/AIDS and their families; Awarded Order of Australia medal in 1994 for 'service to the community as a Palliative Care worker with people suffering with HIV/AIDS'; Founder of *The Tree of Hope*, Pastoral Care and support for PLWHA, their loved ones and carers. R.I.P. (2021)

Monkley, Maureen – Pharmacist St Vincent's Hospital.

Moore, Clover – Lord Mayor of Sydney since 2004; NSW Member for Bligh, 1988-2007; Presenter of NSW Homosexual Anti-Vilification Bill; stoic supporter of gay community throughout AIDS epidemic; Presenter with Tony Carden of Community Forums for PLWHA; Worked with Tony Carden to raise $1 million for 1995 Ward 17 South renovation.

Morgan, Andrew – AIDS activist; worked with ACON. R.I.P. (1995).

Morson, Elizabeth – Mother of early AIDS patient Andrew Morson who nursed her son in the absence of medical support; early victim of homosexual vilification and AIDS discrimination. R.I.P.

Oxford, Marian.

Pollack, Bruce – Theatrical publicist and fund-raiser; Publicist and Director of Mardi Gras for many years; Publicist for other LBTQI+ organisations.

Procter, David – Member of ACT UP.

Raymond, Leigh – Writer and journalist in New York and Sydney during the AIDS pandemic years; Journalist/writer for Sydney GLBTI newspapers and magazines during '80s/'90s.

Roberts, Charles – Founding member of ACT UP Canberra.

Saddington, Lesley – Mother of Tony Carden; Supported Tony during the epidemic; ANKALI volunteer; Author of Tony's biography, *I Don't Want to Talk About It*.

Schey, Linda – Pharmacist, Darlinghurst Sharpe's Pharmacy, helped patients with AIDS medications; Member of ACT UP; ACON HIV Support Project, Positive Speakers Bureau; Hepatitis C Council; Wayside Chapel; Welfare worker with homeless people.

Tietjen, Mark – Bobby Goldsmith Foundation.

Van Reyk – Paul – Early activist with Gay Solidarity Group protesting towards homosexual law reform; AIDS activism with Gay Solidarity Group; First ACON Policy Officer; Safe Sex education organiser; Writer of ACON Manual for Home carers of people with HIV/AIDS; CSN carer; Private Consultant on AIDS policy and programming.

Ward, Colin.

Weaving, Hugo – Actor and former co-actor/director with Tony at Independent Theatre, North Sydney; Contributions in the form of short productions to the Gay and Lesbian Film Festivals; significant contribution against homophobic discrimination with his performance in *Priscilla Queen of the Desert*.

Westmore, Tony – Member of ACT UP.

Whittaker, Bill – President of Sydney Mardi Gras throughout AIDS epidemic; First CEO of ACON; Many years working with HIV Policy and Strategy; Commissioner with UNAIDS High Level Commission on HIV Prevention; Special Representative of National Association of People with HIV (Australia).

Wilkins, David – *Star Observer* journalist; Sister Daisy from Sisters of Perpetual Indulgence.

Wilson, Bridget – Journalist, New Zealand and Fairfax, Sydney; on organising team for Anti-Discrimination Campaign.

Workman, Cassy – Darlinghurst GP who supported many patients during the AIDS epidemic; AIDS medications specialist.

Notes: The above is a list of Tony's original warriors. When Warrior Blood's twentieth anniversary was celebrated in 2014, several had died. They, and those who are known to have passed away since, are acknowledged as R.I.P.

Any warriors without biographies could not be located by the author in 2014.

1996

I'd crossed the chasm, bonded with Tony's other family and felt so changed by our shared journey that to return now to my earlier life would seem meaningless. His *Warrior Blood* message haunted me: 'Will there be more warriors after I'm gone?'

Capital Q interview with Tony about his artwork *Warrior Blood*, 1994.

Early in the New Year I trained to become an Ankali, despite concerns about my appropriateness as an older, heterosexual woman. When I was matched with Anne,[24] the first of the four clients I would support over the following eight years, I knew my decision had been right: Anne, mother of twenty-three-year-old wheelchair-bound Andy,[25] was battling not only the anguish of watching her son struggle with AIDS but also the challenge posed by a husband who saw the disease as God's punishment for the sin of homosexuality. During our two years of weekly meetings I managed to sneak in occasional short interludes with Gerald,[26] who was a keen gardener, to wander amongst his roses and veggies, discussing the joys and challenges of gardening. When an opportunity arose, I'd steer the conversation from pruning and fertilising towards our other shared challenge: having a son with AIDS. Our mutual love of gardens became the catalyst that eventually brought Gerald to Andy's bedside, to hold his son's hand and comfort him as AIDS claimed the life of yet another promising young man.

* * *

For a few months Jane, Phil, Lynna and I had been contemplating what we should do with *Warrior Blood*. Carole Ann's Luncheon Club seemed the ideal home for it, somewhere it could remind the gay community that their warriors were still out there battling on their behalf against AIDS. So I decided to gift it to the club. There it hung until the Luncheon Club closed in 2007, when Carole Ann carefully packed it away and put it into storage.

* * *

---

24 Pseudonym.
25 Pseudonym.
26 Pseudonym.

Tony's other family provided solace, and told me they felt that Tony's story should be told.

They encouraged me to write it lest ACT UP and AIDS fade into history, but grief had engulfed me, so instead I created a garden on my rugged bushland block and planted a peppercorn tree for Tony.

The garden flourished, the peppercorn tree spread its branches and grief's rawness softened into scars to be lived with . . .

I entered my garden into the Australian Open Garden Scheme, and visitors thronged through on pre-arranged weekends. Entry fees were gifted to charity; in my case, an AIDS organisation.

Fred Appleton, a local horticultural colleague of Jim's, who lived locally, was appointed the gatekeeper for the open days. Like the garden, our friendship blossomed and in 2003 Fred and I were married.

2014

'Lesley, do you realise this year will be *Warrior Blood*'s twentieth anniversary?' Carole Ann reminded me seven years later. 'It deserves a celebration. We should put it on display somewhere and get the warriors together for a party.'

As I waited at the Woolloomooloo warehouse where we'd arranged to meet, I wondered where all those years had gone. Carole Ann appeared from a dimly lit corridor pushing a trolley bearing a heavily wrapped package and beaming the welcoming smile I remembered from the Luncheon Club days. Together we gently eased the package to the floor, remembering a dear friend and a lost son.

Like peeling away the years, we folded back layers of bubble wrap, and there it lay, swaddled in the soft white mohair rug she'd wrapped it in, as though it might need not only protection but warmth as it awaited the next chapter in its life. I gazed down at it, hoping that the passage of seven years had been kind. It had.

'It looks perfect, Carole Ann. It's amazing how well it's survived. Thank you for taking such good care of it.'

I hugged her with misty eyes and saw in hers a look of satisfaction and pride that she'd been such a loyal custodian. Later, after we'd carefully loaded the precious and simply framed canvas into my car, we caught up on old times over coffee and cake.

'I think we need a companion catalogue to explain who the warriors are and why Tony chose them,' she suggested. 'It's important we record what it's about because *Warrior Blood* is a significant part of the history of the epidemic. You know, if we can find the warriors and organise it by the time of its anniversary in November we could have a celebration Tony would be proud of.'

I stayed silent, sensing she had something else on her mind.

She continued. 'Young gay men around here often ask me what it was like during the epidemic. They tell me they find it difficult to believe the things they hear. HIV is on the rise again, so it's important they know what really happened. You and I can remember it, but there aren't too many of us left now who do, so it could easily be forgotten. One of us should write about it before it's too late.'

She waited for me to respond but I hesitated, sensing I could be heading towards a fork in the road of my now full and happy retirement life and down a painful path that would take me away from the joys I'd discovered in playing music with others and designing the occasional garden, and lead me back to painful reminders of my son. But I knew already, despite the sacrifices and the challenges, I'd take the detour.

'I'll give it a go, Carole Ann. I'll get started with the catalogue.'

The next day *Warrior Blood* was back at home with me, in the peaceful place I'd nursed my grief surrounded by grey gums, cockatoos and kookaburras. I checked the signatures against the list of fifty-three warriors Carole Ann had prepared, and keen to get started but uncertain where to begin, put it into alphabetical order, contemplating the adventure that lay ahead.

Since 1995 I'd avoided going anywhere near Tony's old haunts. Places like Oxford Street, Woolloomooloo and St Vincent's flooded me with such sadness that I'd allowed them to fade from my memory.

So finding Tony's warriors now would not be easy. I expected there'd be challenges and I realised that if revisiting those years would be difficult for me, how painful might it be for them?

* * *

The sandstone of Sydney's ornate 1880s Town Hall glowed golden in the winter sunshine as I climbed the imposing stairway to the pillared entrance for my appointment with Sydney's Lord Mayor, Clover Moore. Clover had had a high profile as the New South Wales Member of Parliament for the seat of Bligh since 1988. Elected Lord Mayor of Sydney in 2004, Clover is immensely popular because of her conscientious dedication to both roles. Members of Sydney's gay and lesbian community form a large part of her constituency, and they adore Clover because she's served them well, especially during the AIDS epidemic when she fought for their rights in an often-hostile parliament.

Larry Galbraith, former editor of the *Sydney Star Observer*, now Clover's senior policy advisor, greeted me with a warm smile. 'I was a friend of Tony's in the 1990s, and I remember when he was working on *Warrior Blood*. It was an amazing project and poor Tony wasn't well then.'

We talked awhile about the AIDS epidemic and Tony's work with ACT UP.

'Clover has told me about the catalogue, Lesley, and I feel I should warn you about something. When you start talking to people about Tony, you're going to hear a lot of things you probably didn't know. You knew Tony as your son, but to the gay community he would have been another man. What I'm trying to say is that if any of the warriors start going into too much detail you should stop them – just put up your hand and say "too much information".'

I felt uneasy, wondering whether, as his mother, I was the right person to tackle this project. But I'd come this far, and nothing could shake my world more than Tony's death already had. If I discovered anything about him in death that I hadn't known about him in life, then so be it.

Clover invited me into her spacious office: green carpet, deep cedar chairs, dark wood desk. Light streamed in through softly draped windows.

'It's lovely to see you again, Lesley. It's been almost twenty years and you've hardly changed at all.'

She was the Clover I remembered, gracious and ever diplomatic. Her hairstyle had changed in keeping with a new era, but she still wore a choker around her elegant neck. Tea arrived on a tray, and we sat at the coffee table to talk.

'I enjoyed working with Tony so much,' she recalled. 'He was so passionate and determined, always such a loyal friend. That zany sense of humour of his always made us laugh even when the going got tough.'

When I told her about the catalogue she was very supportive, and even offered me access to her personal files from the era, now held at the State Library of NSW. At the end of our meeting, Clover promised she'd send me her photograph and a profile piece for the *Warrior Blood* catalogue, and Larry said he would email me whatever contact details he could find for other warriors. Clover checked her watch, the clock in the tower chimed, and I knew it was time to leave. The ball was now rolling. Clover was the first of Tony's warriors I could tick off my list. Only fifty-two to go.

I decided to tackle next the warriors I already knew: Will, Lyle and Claude. They could be my guinea pigs before I ventured into less familiar territory.

Those who had lived through the AIDS crisis of the eighties and nineties had been left with indelible memories, which they had often chronicled in paintings and sculpture, photography, books and plays and occasionally music. The era had been rich in artistic expression.

A few weeks later, I received an invitation, through Larry, to attend the premier of Lyle Chan's string quartet *An AIDS Activist's Memoir in Music* at the ABC's city auditorium.

Memories triggered by the music, from the horns, cymbals and police whistles reminiscent of ACT UP's stormier exploits to the sweetly poignant flutes and strings of the movements 'Et Tu Bruce' and 'Tony-ony Macaroni', came flooding back and had me on the edge of my seat, often choking back tears.

Afterwards, as Lyle frantically signed CDs for ardent fans, I managed to get a word in about my new project, the *Warrior Blood* catalogue. We arranged to meet at the Tilbury Hotel in Woolloomooloo, around the corner from Tony's former Crystal House, in a week's time.

I felt apprehensive as I contemplated walking the footpaths I'd trodden with Tony and visiting our old haunt The Tilbury, where we'd dined, laughed and sung together. So I was relieved when dear Fred, my husband of the past eleven years, announced, 'You're going to need some help with this project. I really don't like to think of you wandering around the inner city on your own. Someone like you could be pretty vulnerable.'

It was clear what he meant, although I didn't like admitting it. I looked at his broad shoulders and heavy grey moustache and felt reassured. No mugger would risk attacking me with Fred by my side. I hugged him, relieved to have an accomplice.

'It makes me very sad that I never knew Tony,' he reflected.

* * *

Lyle was readily recognisable among the other customers whiling away the afternoon in the dappled shade at the Tilbury's outdoor tables. He assured me with a warm smile that he didn't mind if I recorded our meeting so I placed my tape recorder on the table and switched it on while Fred retreated to the bar for a bottle of wine and three glasses.

We reminisced about the ups and downs of the nineties, and about Tony. Lyle's role as a spokesperson for ACT UP, ACON and NAPWHA (National Association of People with HIV Australia) enabled him to provide contact details for more warriors and, even better, to remember what they'd been doing when Tony had coerced them into giving their blood. *What a headstart this is*, I thought gratefully, as Lyle racked his brain and I hurriedly jotted down names and notes.

'Thank you, Lyle, that should get me started,' I said, sitting back to peruse the list and savour the wine. 'By the way, do you remember *Acacius (Stigmata)*?'

'Of course I do,' he replied. 'I remember it from Tony's wake. What a wonderful portrait, iconic too. Wasn't it hanging in St Vincent's AIDS ward?'

'Well, it was, but it's had a rather chequered history since then and now I have both *Acacius (Stigmata)* and *Warrior Blood* at home. I've been thinking about what to do with them. It's no use me being their custodian. They'd be in safer and better hands elsewhere – maybe in a gallery or a museum. After all, they really belong to the gay community and they're an important part of the history of the epidemic. What do you think?'

'What an amazing coincidence, Lesley, because I bumped into Ted Gott last July at the International AIDS Conference in Melbourne and Ted asked me if I had any idea where *Warrior Blood* and *Acacius (Stigmata)* had got to. He'd been hoping to get hold of them for the conference. You remember Ted – he was curator of the "Art in the Age of AIDS" exhibition at the National Gallery.'

My heart leapt and sank at the same time. The artworks had missed the conference but now they'd find a new purpose. I made a note to call Ted Gott.

For the remainder of the year I chased up warriors, from Darlinghurst to Melbourne, Canberra to Darwin, even overseas. Many willingly supplied material for their 'profiles': a photograph, a page or so about how they'd met Tony, how they'd been involved in the epidemic, and the background that had placed them there. A few people found revisiting their memories and writing about those years too painful, so instead they agreed to meet with me and talk about them over coffee or lunch. They didn't mind if I recorded our conversation, but they preferred to leave the writing to me.

Towards the end of the year Professor Cooper contacted me. 'Lesley, would you be able to lay your hands on *Warrior Blood*?' he asked. 'We'd like to have it on display at St Vincent's for World AIDS Day and later in the week at a celebration for the thirtieth anniversary of the original AIDS ward. We'd really appreciate it if you could bring it in.'

* * *

In the rambling garden of St Vincent's Palliative Care Clinic invited guests, including many of the warriors, sipped champagne as they mingled and chatted before the evening's official formalities began. Displayed on a huge wooden easel was *Warrior Blood*, with side panels listing the fifty-three 'warriors' and describing the contributions they'd made during the epidemic. The warriors crowded around it, finding their names and renewing old friendships.

The following day *Warrior Blood* and its catalogue were borne proudly across Victoria Street to St Vincent's Hospital, to be displayed in the Infectious Diseases Clinic that had replaced Ward 17 South since AIDS had become a treatable disease.

'I've hung Tony's collage in the patients' waiting room,' John, the clinic manager, told me later. 'It's been a great source of interest to our patients. In fact, they often say how surprised they are to discover that only two decades ago things were so different for people living with AIDS. When they read the *Catalogue of Warriors* they're surprised to learn of the challenges the warriors faced to keep people like themselves alive.'

We agreed that although the Infectious Diseases Clinic was the most suitable place for *Warrior Blood* to be displayed at present, in time, as combination therapy reduced the clinic's work, *Warrior Blood* should be handed over to a more appropriate gallery or museum.

Chapter 27

Pilgrimage

2015

Twelve years had passed since *Acacius (Stigmata)*'s rejection by St Vincent's but my anger still remained, resurging whenever discrimination raised its malevolent head. I called Ted Gott. 'I was very sorry to hear from Lyle that you'd been looking for *Acacius (Stigmata)* and *Warrior Blood*,' I confessed to Ted, 'because I have both of them at my home.' I could sense his relief.

'Yes, we wondered what had become of them,' he replied. 'They're significant artworks and I'd like to see them in a gallery somewhere, where the public can appreciate them. That way they would also be accessible whenever they're needed for another event like the AIDS conference.'

The next day I shuffled the furniture in my living room around to make space to photograph the artistic heritage Tony had left me, a heritage that would now be recognised, thanks to Ted Gott. I studied the two works from my blue chair while I pondered Ted's words. The dilemma now was which galleries I should approach.

After considering the many suggestions that had rolled in from family, warriors and members of the gay community about *Acacius (Stigmata)*, I eventually contacted Angus Trumble, Director of the National Portrait Gallery. Thus began several months of negotiation during which I provided the requisite documentation, including the painting's provenance, a short biography of Tony with particular focus on his ACT UP years and finally the artist's approval, which AñA was only too happy to supply.

I watched as two couriers carefully wrapped the precious portrait in layers of felt and bubble wrap and loaded it into their van for the journey to its new home in Canberra – Australia's National Portrait Gallery. As the van disappeared around the corner, I felt as apprehensive for the artwork's safe passage as I had for Tony on his first day at school.

Acacius (Stigmata) – Portrait of Tony Carden joined the gallery's main exhibition throughout the following year, when close to two million visitors, including many from the gay community, made their way to Canberra to view the portraits of Australians of note and to read about their achievements.

* * *

On a brisk, blue-sky October morning, Phil, Jane, Lynna, Fred and I made a family pilgrimage to Canberra. We gathered at the National Portrait Gallery to rediscover and to farewell our son and brother, bursting with pride for his achievements, heartbroken that we'd lost him, but satisfied that at last, in his guise as Saint Acacius, he had found a safe, well-earned resting-place.

Phil spotted him first and beckoned us to join the group of curious viewers gathered around the eye-catching portrait. They whispered in amazement as they read the side panels about Tony's and ACT UP's achievements during the AIDS epidemic and AñA's account of the context of the work's creation.

Angus Trumble related the portrait's history in the gallery's magazine:

> Artist AñA Wojak remembers Tony Carden as a handsome young man of unusual warmth, gentleness and generosity,

combined with fierce determination – a beautiful soul. They kept in touch after *Acacius (Stigmata)* was finished, and in the middle of a Sunday afternoon excursion to the Hawkesbury, Tony came across an old scythe – no doubt remembering the original 1987 grim-reaper public-health AIDS awareness campaign. Tony picked it up and gave it to AñA, a typically theatrical gesture with a hint of mischievous gallows humour.

When at length he died of AIDS in 1995 at the age of thirty-three, more than 400 people attended Tony Carden's funeral, and AñA Wojak arranged for the painting to be displayed prominently at the wake, which took place afterwards in a crowded gallery in Glebe. On that occasion a general consensus immediately formed that *Acacius (Stigmata)* ought to belong in Ward 17 South at St. Vincent's 'in recognition of the gay and lesbian community's struggle for acceptance and dignity for people living (and dying) with HIV/AIDS, and as a source of inspiration and comfort to patients.'

In due course the painting was formally presented to and accepted by the hospital at an amply publicised morning tea. Some years later, however, the painting was returned, wrapped in a hospital-issue cotton blanket, to Tony Carden's mother, Lesley Saddington, apparently because some members of the hospital's board strongly objected to the portrayal of a gay man as a catholic saint. Evidently it had not yet occurred to them that Wojak's painting could be seen, even more compellingly, as the portrayal of a catholic saint as a young gay man, full of promise, with blond hair cut à la Depeche Mode, and a knack for getting a lot of important things done in what little time he knew he had left.

Angus Trumble, Director, National Portrait Gallery of Australia, extract from the article 'Stigma Stigmata', *Portrait*, Winter Edition, 2015.

Beside Tony was Eddie Mabo, champion of Indigenous and Torres Strait land rights, and around the corner in an adjoining gallery, a death-mask of Ned Kelly, in a glass case. 'Tony's in good company,' remarked Phil, winking at Ned.

* * *

Later in the year I contacted Sydney's Powerhouse Ultimo: the Museum of Applied Arts and Sciences, to offer *Warrior Blood* as part of its collection of AIDS epidemic memorabilia. Tony's brave warriors took their place beside the Memorial Quilt, in the museum's permanent collection, and as such are now the property of the Australian people.

Let this truth set our children free

The voices we most need to hear in response to the child abuse royal commission's final report are those that have been silenced forever. What would they say, the child abuse victims who didn't survive, the men and women who were unable to bear the pain and have taken their own lives? They would almost certainly share the gratitude shown by survivors of childhood sexual assaults that the story has been told at last . . .

The findings should fall heavily on all the organisations whose response to cases of child abuse has been defective . . .

. . . the best monument to the dead is to ensure the practices exposed by this commission never recur.

Editorial, *The Sydney Morning Herald*, 15 December 2017

Epilogue

> My brother Phil remains. God gave him to me. His truth and care make my eyes tear. For him I leave my candle burning.
>
> Tony's journal, 1995

1996

It was a spring afternoon a year after Tony had died, and ten years since Andrew's death. Elizabeth and I sat beneath the cape chestnut in the garden at Karingal, reminiscing about our lost sons. Elizabeth ventured softly, in her usual dreamy way, 'Did Tony ever tell you what happened to him and Andrew in prep school? Andrew told me.'

'Told you what?' I had no idea about where this might be leading.

'Andrew told me they'd been sexually abused by one of the teachers. Well, he didn't put it quite that way. He said one of the teachers, Lance Edwards,[27] had taught some of the boys – including himself and Tony – homosexual acts. You'd remember him, Lesley. He taught music and he used to take them in his car sometimes to rugby or to buy them something from the shops at lunch time. In those days, it seemed fairly harmless.'

I sank into my chair, a nauseous chill spreading through me. I was shocked, in disbelief. Those poor boys! So young, so easily influenced, so innocent and so helpless against evil. What a calamitous introduction to their sexuality. I put imaginary arms around my son, to hold him close, to comfort his spirit as I apologised to him.

---

27 Pseudonym.

So that was Tony's secret, the horror he'd harboured all those years. The 'It' he'd refused to talk about. At last I understood: the panic attacks, the nightmares, why he'd planned to kill himself, why he'd left Australia and lost his trust in others. By comparison the challenges of my own early years had been child's play.

I seethed. How could any man, especially someone in a position of trust, so betray his charges? Had Lance Edwards been standing there at that moment, I'd have a ripped him to shreds like a clawing, foaming-at-the-mouth tigress. Of the many possibilities for Tony's torment I'd considered, this was something I could never have imagined.

'Perhaps, had we known earlier . . .' reflected Elizabeth, 'but it's too late now.'

* * *

Years later, after time had tempered the impact of Elizabeth's revelation, several former Pennryn pupils went to the police to register charges of sexual abuse against a number of the school's teachers, one of whom was Lance Edwards. The police set up an official investigation, and called for members of the public with any information to contact them. Amazed and shocked to realise that there'd been others as well as Tony and Andrew, I admired the men's courage to have at last come forward, and I deduced that two of the boys were Tony's and Andrew's contemporaries. Elizabeth had recently died, which meant of course that the evidence she could have provided about our sons' abuse was lost, and that my own evidence now amounted to little more than hearsay. Nevertheless I was considering what input I could offer on Andrew's and Tony's behalf when an out-of-the-blue phone call put me on alert.

'Hello Lesley, this is Leonie Clarke.[28] I've just heard about Tony. I'm so sorry to hear that he has died.'

---

28 Pseudonym.

'I appreciate your thoughts, Leonie, but that was fourteen years ago,' I replied, remembering Leonie from my time in horticulture. Decades ago she'd taught me botany but apart from petals, pods and photosynthesis we'd had little in common, certainly not husbands, children or schools. I wondered why she'd contacted me now – why this sudden interest in Tony?

'Let's meet for a coffee and a chat about old times at Pennryn, and about Tony,' she offered.

Intrigued, I accepted her invitation and met her at a coffee shop near a local railway station overlooking a row of liquidambar trees. As we casually sipped our coffee, I wondered what had prompted this contact from her after so many years. Surely she was fishing for something. I'd already nailed her as an inexperienced angler because she'd offered no bait. Then, with the autumn leaves fluttering by the window, Leonie got down to brass tacks.

'Didn't Tony have some kind of trouble with a teacher when he was at Pennryn? I seem to remember something . . .'

I smelt the rat (or fish?) and thought, *Ha! The police investigation!*

I played along, curious to see where this would lead, and described Tony's prep school traumas and how I'd learnt from Elizabeth about Lance Edwards and his extra-curricular tuition. For good measure I threw in mention of Mark Young's 'after-school lessons' and my disgust at the way Dr Hastings[29] had dismissed my concerns as those of 'an over-anxious mother'.

At the mention of Mark, her eyes flickered so I guessed he was the fish she was angling for. 'But you wouldn't go to the police, would you? Pennryn is such a great school. I'm actually on the executive of the school's Parent's Association, and I do some coaching there as well, so I know what excellent educational standards Pennryn has. It would be a great shame to see the school's reputation sullied over something that happened so long ago.'

---

29 Pseudonym.

No, I thought, *it wouldn't be a shame, Leonie, it would damned-well be the right thing to do.* I'd been unaware of her connection with the school, and nor did it interest me, but I did remember that she was a conscientious, churchgoing Presbyterian, so her easy deviousness surprised me. However, her message was loud and clear, and I visualised her at the next school council meeting divulging that Lesley Saddington could possibly be a person of concern regarding her late son Tony Carden. I didn't realise it at the time, but that's exactly how the school council saw me.

As soon as I arrived home I phoned the police. I was connected to a matter-of-fact female detective who was working on the enquiry and related my evidence to add to what the police already knew about Lance Edwards and Pennryn.

* * *

The Royal Commission into Institutional Responses to Child Sexual Abuse was a legacy of Australia's first female prime minister, Julia Gillard, and a feisty, fearless leader she was, standing her ground against the misogyny that was regularly hurled at her across the floor of Australia's federal parliament. Julia called out the sexist abuse for what it was and denounced her abusers. Tony would have cheered her on as a fellow warrior.

In mid-2014, when hearings into Sydney's private schools were being planned, Pennryn's turn finally arrived. I noticed an announcement about it in the morning paper: 'Royal Commission to Hold Public Hearing into Xxxxx. Any person who believes that they have a direct and substantial interest in the scope and purpose of the public hearing is invited to lodge a written application . . .'

After a few days raking through scattered memories, I took up my pen and, choosing my words carefully, recounted the two occasions on which I believed Pennryn had failed in its duty of care towards Tony and hence also to us, his parents: as an eleven-year-old, by prep school teacher Lance Edwards, and as a fifteen-year-old, by senior school teacher Mark Young. I described the events as I remembered them, pointing out that I was completely blind to their significance at the time. I also recounted my meeting with Leonie Clarke.

Two weeks later, a representative from the Royal Commission contacted me. 'We've received your statement, Mrs Saddington. Would you like to appear before the hearing? If you're planning to appear you'll need a solicitor . . .'

Me? Appear? Solicitor? My response should have been a resounding 'yes', but imagining a manipulative barrister revelling in making mincemeat of me as the school's legal eagles twisted my evidence, I replied, 'If you think I could be helpful, I'd be willing to appear, but it's not something I'd otherwise choose to do.'

Jelly legs, tummy butterflies and a limited budget won the day along with relief at being out of the limelight rather than in it.

Several months later the hearing into Pennryn began. I sat at home in my blue wing chair, laptop on my knees, Bombon, my American bulldog, at my feet, steeling myself for the twenty-one days of proceedings that lay ahead. Considering myself a mere observer, I'd decided not to travel to and from the city to sit in a gallery, hear things that might upset me and eat sandwiches all alone in a soulless Pitt Street café. Besides, I had moral support at hand. Phil was observing too, working from his home while keeping an eye on the proceedings, and only a phone call away.

The more I heard, as the days passed, the more sadness and despair were compounded on top of the grief I already felt over what Tony had endured during his school years.

One after another they stood before the commissioner to reveal what for decades had remained hidden from public scrutiny – men in their fifties, who until now had kept their sinister secrets to themselves, as had Tony. They'd been prepubescent boys back then, innocent, naïve, carefree schoolchildren.

They delivered their victim impact statements, recounted their stories of abuse, some haltingly between sobs, others restraining their anger as they relived events that had changed their lives forever. A few, in fear of breaking down, had a friend read their statement while they stood by, downcast, ashamed. As the inquiry ground on, I learnt the reasons why they'd never spoken of it: they'd thought it was their fault; they'd thought they'd be blamed, even punished; they'd thought no-one would believe them; they'd presumed they'd be ostracised by their peers . . .

Like Tony, they'd remained silent.

Almost without exception, as soon as they could, they'd fled the scene of their abuse – some had moved interstate, many overseas, as had Tony. And they were the ones who'd survived. Others had taken their own lives. We heard on their behalf from shattered parents who spoke of sons lost to substance abuse and suicide, all former students of Pennryn, Tony's schoolmates. As these evils came to light, I understood the torment he'd struggled with, his nightmares and panic attacks, why he'd fled his home and country. Now that his secret was out, Phil and I believed that Tony would expect us to take up his sword and fight on his behalf, as warriors for justice.

Overwhelmed by grief, anger and frustration, I exploded into an outburst of wrath that found its way onto paper. I emailed my emotive missive to the letters section at *The Sydney Morning Herald*, to add to tales from the Royal Commission already delivering daily headlines. Two days later my letter appeared in the weekend edition:

> I listen to the Royal Commission . . . and I weep for those men whose lives have been damaged by people into whose care they were entrusted. I'm also very angry.
>
> My son Tony Carden (who died at 33) was one such man. Tony was abused on two occasions and it is painful to accept what is now revealed. We were (mis)led to believe that Xxxxx would guide our sons along the road to manhood inspired by the school's motto, Xxxx Xxxx – Do the Honourable Thing.

Epilogue

> I believe my son was 'groomed' in the junior school and that thereafter the die was cast. ('A sapling can be bent as by an ill wind.' Morris West, *The Devil's Advocate*). Xxxxx accepted our trust and our money and in return damaged our sons, their psyches and their concept of sexuality. Xxxxx has lost its moral compass. When a product proves faulty a refund is in order. Xxxxx should refund school fees to all those families whose sons have been victims of the school's lack of vigilance.
>
> I would gladly put my refund towards an education program for students so that this never happens again.
>
> Lesley Saddington, The Sydney Morning Herald, 25 February 2015

No sooner had I read myself in print than the phone began to ring with call after call, from parents remembering Tony, his former school friends, and a TV program director who invited me to appear on the ABC's *7.30 Report*.

Most of the phone calls were sympathetic and supportive but reflecting on Leonie Clarke's 2009 fishing expedition I responded warily, particularly regarding the *7.30 Report*.

As victims were cross-examined, a picture emerged from their statements, revealing how Xxxxx had gone about baiting his prey.

From one witness:

> Xxxxx was well liked by the students at Xxxxx because he always made classroom activities fun. I thought he was a bit too hands-on, as he would often tickle or touch students, including me. The tickling usually involved Xxxxx tickling me all over my body. When I was being tickled, he'd start on my torso and hover over me in a way that would obscure him from the other boys in the classroom. As he tickled, his hands would move down my body to my genitals, at which point he would slow down and cup my penis on the outside of my clothes. As he was doing this, he'd be laughing and joking, which made it all

seem acceptable and okay. This happened to me at least every second day throughout year five (aged ten/eleven). As the year went on, Xxxxx became more confident in what he was doing to me. During the tickling incidents, Xxxxx began to take opportunities to move his hands inside my shorts and underwear, and touch me on the penis, skin to skin. He would then touch, stroke and cup my genitals in a sexual way. Sometimes, when he was doing this, I would flinch and he would have less opportunity to grope me, usually keeping his hands outside my pants.

From another:

Xxxxx was known by the boys as 'a tickler'. Some boys quickly pitched to what he was really doing. He used his tickling-technique to 'feel' the bodies of boys he'd set his sights on, literally. Oh, he'd laugh and pretend it was all a game, but it was a way of conditioning a boy to the idea that it was OK, that it was all part of his tickling game to start around the ribs, move to the waist then down the thighs, tickling and massaging as he moved lower until he reached the groin where his hand would reach between the boys legs to cradle his genitals, gently the first time, then on ensuing occasions more firmly. He'd laugh all the while as the 'game' progressed, trying to make the whole exercise appear light-hearted and then, if the boy hadn't told him to 'get out' or 'leave me alone' or 'I don't like it', one day his hand might just slip inside the boy's shorts to repeat the game skin-to-skin until he'd manage to stroke the boy's penis and scrotum. Some boys, usually the more aggressive ones, would have managed to escape by this time, but there were others, perhaps quieter, shyer boys, who'd either tolerate the 'game' and get away afterwards as fast as they could, or not dare to resist. Others thought they'd done something to deserve the treatment . . .

And another:

> While we were getting changed for sport Xxxxx would watch us, then he'd approach a number of the boys while they were naked and try to tickle and touch them. At showering time all the boys would use the showers. Xxxxx would always appear. The showers were all open and there was no privacy. Xxxxx would stand in the doorway watching us.

And another:

> The playground was busy and I was running past Xxxxx at a distance of about five metres when Xxxxx said to me something like:
> 'Your shirt needs to be tucked in. Come here.'
> He then took hold of my shirt and tucked it down the front of my shorts. He tucked his hand inside my underpants and cupped it over my genitals and pressed against them for a short period. The next time it happened he reached behind me and tucked my shirt into my underpants from behind. He slipped fingers between my buttocks and inserted his finger into my rectum. He held it there for a short period while I squirmed and cried out. He was rough and assertive. I was a small child and unable to resist or defend myself. I felt immediate pain and bled from my rectum for several days.

When one witness revealed what had taken place at Xxxxx's trial in 2009, I realised just how far society had yet to go to deal appropriately with paedophilia:

> The trial of Xxxxx in 2009 was a joke of the most serious proportions. The courtroom was moved at the last minute and when we arrived there was a very small space to wait. Xxxxx was

standing no more than two metres away. I found this very distressing. The judge lauded Xxxxx on his punctuality and his neatness of presentation. She (the judge) decided that Xxxxx had faced enough vilification over his actions and that was punishment enough. I got up and walked out as she slapped him on the wrist with a good behaviour bond which I now know to be a suspended sentence (of his four-year sentence).

* * *

During the hearing's last few days, when we thought we'd heard the worst of it, the second incident of Tony's abuse took the spotlight. And now it was the headmaster's turn in the witness box. Evidence in the form of a 'letter' the headmaster had written for his records in 1992 was presented and tabled. There it was, in black and white, bearing his signature: evidence that in 1973 not only had he been aware of Xxxxx's abuse of two boys, one of whom I deduced to be Tony, but also – and here came the bombshell – that someone (whom I recognised despite the use of pseudonyms to have been one of Tony's school-friends) was planning to sue Pennryn over Lance Edwards' abuse; that if the school didn't pay up he'd reveal the fact that another teacher, referred to as 'ARD', had had a two-year-long 'affair' with a fifteen-year-old student: 'Everyone knew, we'd seen them.'

I assumed, due to the fact that no hint of the scandal had ever emerged, that the school must have paid up.

The headmaster had made the contents known to only a select group in the hope that the matter could be dampened down.

With some difficulty and help from a former schoolfriend of Tony, now a barrister, I managed to have Tony's pseudonym removed so that what I'd complained about to the headmaster in 1977 was now out in the open. It was also revealed that the files of two boys had strangely disappeared from the school's files – the only files that had ever gone missing. One was Tony's.

Epilogue

Phil rang me: 'We all knew what Mark Young was up to when Tony was fifteen,' he said, 'and now it's been exposed. And you and Keith both went to the headmaster about it when it was happening. He's lying.'

I now realised that in deciding not to appear before the commission, I'd unwittingly made a huge mistake. I regretted not having appeared because I could have confronted Dr Hastings and he'd not have dared call me an 'overanxious mother' a second time around.

Realising the significance of our evidence, Phil and I applied for a Private Hearing. Only then did I discover the burden Phil had borne because of his brother's abuse. Light was being shed at last on how the two brothers had kept hidden a dark secret. I listened, heartbroken, as Phil presented his evidence to the Commissioner.

Phil revealed that he'd become his brother's confidante when Tony was eleven. Tony had sworn him to secrecy, a promise Phil had honoured, until now. 'One day in 1973 I saw Tony rush down to the old toilet at the end of our back garden. He went in and slammed the door. I wondered what he was up to, so I followed him, banged on the door and asked him. He came out, pulled down his pants and showed me a rash around his genitals. He was very upset.

'Look, Phil. I think I've caught the pox or something. Do you know what this is?'

I told him I had no idea what it was and said he should show it to a doctor.

How could Tony, as an eleven-year-old, have visited a doctor without my help? I remembered the cold sores he'd developed around the same time, connected them to the rash and traced the whole thing back to Edwards.

Phil continued: 'A few months later Tony told me he was planning to kill himself. I didn't really believe him because, knowing Tony, I thought it was probably just a bit of attention-seeking. Then one afternoon I happened to walk past Jane's bedroom door and I saw Tony with one end of his dressing-gown cord around his neck and the other end tied to the high headboard of Jane's bed. He threw himself out and down off the bed, and as I rushed in he landed on the floor because thank God Jane's bed wasn't high enough. I picked him up and sat him on the bed and gave him a strong talking-to. I told Keith about it and we agreed not to tell you, Mum, because we didn't want to get you upset.'

Upset? What had they taken me for? My heart ached. My tears flowed.

After we'd presented our evidence, the Commissioner told us that many sexual abuse victims eventually break their silence, usually when they reach their sixties, finally able to talk about something they've harboured for most of their lives. I thought of Tony, how he might have looked at sixty and wondered whether he'd have followed suit.

Strangely, most of the perpetrators, including those the Royal Commission had found guilty, were never brought to trial. Why? I'll never know the answer to that. Nor will I ever know what might have happened had Tony remained in Australia and studied at NIDA. Would he be alive today, working as an actor and/or a director of repute? And what might he have become had he not suffered any abuse?

I will never know.

* * *

Bibliography

ACON: 1992 – 1996, Annual Reports

ACT UP New York: 1988, Poster *The Government Has Blood On Its Hands*, New York Public Library

ACT UP Sydney Archives: 2015, State Library of NSW, Sydney (with permission)

Aldrich, Robert (editor): 2006, *Gay life and Culture, A World History*, Thames and Hudson Ltd., London

Borten, Craig and Wallack, Melissa: 2013, *Dallas Buyers Club*

Carden, Tony: 1994, *Warrior Blood*, Blood swatches on canvas, Work in Progress

Carden, Tony: 1995, *Notes of an AIDS Victim*, Tony's Journal

Chan, Lyle: 2015, *Warrior Blood* – Lyle's Warrior Profile as in *Catalogue of Warriors*

Chan, Lyle: 2013, *An Activist's Memoir in Music* – Composer's notes

Dunbar, Jamie: 2024, Photographs courtesy of Jamie Dunbar, www.jamiedunbar.com

Eliot, T.S.: 1967, *Murder in the Cathedral*, Faber and Faber, London

Glover, Richard: 2019, November 10th, *Sydney Morning Herald*, Weekend Spectrum

Gott, Ted: 1994, *Don't leave Me This Way – Art in the Age of AIDS*, The Craftsman Press, Melbourne

HIV Treatment In Australia – 2015, A Brief History

Hunt, Simon: 1995, *Eulogy for Tony Carden*

Kirby, The Honourable Justice Michael: 1988, *Insights from the Stockholm Conference*

Kramer, Larry: 1983, *1,112 and Counting*, New York Native, Issue 59, 1983

Kramer, Larry: 1978, *Faggots*, Grove Press, New York

Lost Gay Sydney: 2015, *Lost Gay Sydney's* Crisis Chronology, www.camp.org.au

MedBroadcast.com: 2017, *Human Herpes virus 8*

Moore, Clover: Clover Moore Archives, State Library of NSW, Sydney (with permission)

NAPHWA; 2014, *Through Our Eyes*, edited by John Rule, National Association of People with HIV Australia

Ogden, Russell D: 1994, *Euthanasia and Assisted Suicide in Persons With Acquired Immunodeficiency Syndrome (AIDS)*, Simon Fraser University, National Library of Canada

Royal Commission into Institutional Responses to Child Sexual Abuse Case Study (details protected): Public Hearing, Daily Transcripts (dates protected); Report; Findings

Sendziuk, Paul: 2003, *Learning to Trust*, UNSW Press, Sydney

Shilts, Randy: 1988, *And the Band Played On*, St Martins Press, New York

Sydney Star Observer: 2015, 1991-1995 archives

The Albion Centre: 2005, *A HIV/AIDS Timeline*, The Albion Centre, Surry Hills, Sydney

The Australian: 1995, Obituaries

The New York Times: *The AIDS Epidemic 1988-1990*; www.nytimes.com 1991-1993; www.nytimes.com.aids.timeline; www.nytimes.com.aids.timeline 1994-1997

The Star Observer: October 1995, Archives, Kirsty Machon quote; 1993, Archives, Photo and article, AIDS Antidiscrimination Campaign; 1995, Photo of Clover Moore, Tony Carden and Michael Glynn, Darlinghurst; 1993, Archives, Article 'Anti-racist Ethics'

The Sydney Morning Herald: 1991-2017, archives@sydneymorningherald.com

The Tribune Australia: 1961, Editorial, Australia, per Trove

Trumble, Angus: 2015, *Stigma Stigmata*, Portrait Magazine, Winter Edition, National Portrait Gallery, Canberra

West, Morris: 2017, *The Devil's Advocate*, Allen and Unwin, Sydney

Williams, Tennessee: 1976, *Cat on a Hot Tin Roof and Other Plays*, Penguin Books, London

Wojak, Aña: 1991, *Acacius (Stigmata) – Portrait of Tony Carden*, National Portrait Gallery, Canberra

Acknowledgements

Tony's story has had a long gestation and many have nurtured it throughout its journey.

In 1995 after Tony died, his friends and fellow warriors suggested that the story of his life as actor, artist and activist and of ACT UP's achievements 'needed to be told' and that I should write it. Had it been written then, it would have differed significantly from the story that has since unfolded.

With grief too raw and memories too painful to re-live, the years drifted by until 2013 when Carole Ann King, of Luncheon Club fame and custodian of Tony's artwork *Warrior Blood*, took the historical blood-collage out of storage and contacted me, reminding me that 2014 would be *Warrior Blood*'s twentieth anniversary.

Carole Ann suggested there should be a Warrior's twenty-year reunion celebration and that it would be a good idea to prepare a Catalogue of Warriors so that the project's history would be preserved. The collation of the catalogue became the next chapter in Tony's story.

Carole Ann also reflected that with so few people remaining who had lived through the AIDS epidemic, as had she and I, perhaps one of us should write about it, lest its history be lost to future generations.

I pondered this and accepting that Tony's and ACT UP's stories are indeed a significant part of that history, agreed to write about it, after I'd finished collating the *Warrior Blood* catalogue. Thank you Carole Ann for your foresight and encouragement, the reason this story has at last been written.

Meeting the Warriors and hearing their poignant stories took me back to the years of HIV/AIDS. It jogged many memories and provided a foundation for the research that was necessary to set Tony's story into the wider framework of Sydney's AIDS epidemic. Thank you, brave warriors, especially Julie Bates AO, Don Baxter, Andrew Bredin, Lyle Chan, David Crawford, Will Conyers, Frances Dart, Ross Duffin, Jamie Dunbar, Claude Fabian, C. Moore Hardy, Kirsty Machon, the late Sister Margaret Mines OAM, Lord Mayor-Councillor Clover Moore AO, Bruce Pollack, Leigh Raymond, Bill Whittaker and the thirty-seven other Warriors whose memories were sometimes too painful to recount. Your reluctance revealed the lingering pathos of those years.

But it was the revelations of the 2015 Royal Commission into Institutional Responses to Child Sexual Abuse in that brought fire to my pen.

When the appalling truth was revealed about what lay behind Tony's childhood suicide attempt, what it was that he'd refused to talk about, I at last understood the reason for his passion to fight for the rights of others. I also understood how anger about his own abuse had turned a damaged boy into a determined activist.

Thank you Julia Gillard.

Special thanks are due to Tony's fellow ACT UP members: Ross Duffin, who not only encouraged me to write Tony's story, but having worked with ACON during the '90s, also provided anecdotes and information that confirmed and enhanced many of my hazy memories of those years; Lyle Chan, whose knowledge of AIDS medications enabled many to survive, helped me with contact details for many of Tony's Warriors, also provided the information that ensured that the two artworks, *Acacius (Stigmata) Portrait of Tony Carden* and *Warrior Blood*, were ultimately delivered into the right hands and through his moving string quartet *An AIDS Memoir in Music* expressed his memories of Bruce Brown and 'Tony-ony Macaroni' with evocative eloquence; Claude Fabian, whose enthusiasm for the project knew no bounds, extending from proof-reading early forms of the manuscript to hosting memorable lunches organised to introduce me to others

Acknowledgements

whose input would prove invaluable; Kirsty Machon whose imagination and organising skills ensured that ACT UP's protests, of necessity unrehearsed, always proceeded hitchlessly. I also acknowledge with gratitude my friend Luise Di Corpo, whose patient and ongoing editing of the evolving manuscript proved invaluable.

When artist AñA Wojak compassionately decided to display the painting *Acacius (Stigmata) – Portrait of Tony Carden, 1994*, at Tony's wake in 1995, its future journey via St Vincent's Hospital to Canberra's National Portrait Gallery was unwittingly set in motion. AñA also provided the portrait's background story and its creative technical details. The LGBTQI+ community and I gratefully extend our thanks, AñA.

Soon after the manuscript's first draft was completed, Tony's friend and co-activist, Julie Bates OAM, introduced me to Alison Fraser, Book Therapy, for editing and possible publication. Julie, your support has been sterling and continuous, including having facilitated my liaison with Positive Life's Nick Parkhill and Jane Costello and having organised the reading of a chapter of *I Don't Want to Talk About it* at Sydney's 2023 Candlelight Memorial Service.

My grateful and ongoing thanks for your support, Julie.

Alison's initial appraisal of the manuscript was enthusiastic and after editing and re-editing it herself, Alison arranged for professional editor Samantha Kent to undertake final editing and styling. Thank you Samantha for your expertise.

Alison also advised me to seek a legal defamation opinion.

Peter Karp of Karp O'Neill Lawyers read the manuscript and briefed Barrister Hannah Ryan (Eleven Wentworth) whose advice provided peace of mind. Thank you, Hannah.

Peter, your support to me since 2015 as the mother of a sexually abused child and the subsequent writer of his story has been comforting and reassuring. Thank you Peter, for being the right person in the right place at the right times.

Alison's plan to publish this book herself was unexpectedly thwarted, for health reasons, but despite this Alison, you have remained there, ever loyal to me, to Tony and to the message of his story, as you handed the publishing into the capable hands of Michael Hanrahan and Anna Clemann of Publish Central. My sincere thanks to you, Alison.

I extend my gratitude to the Publish Central team, who seamlessly transformed my manuscript into this book and also to my Publicist, Aisling Brady, who has conveyed its availability to you, its readers.

Tony's story acquired encouragement from an unexpected source by way of the Postcard Pen Pal Project, a Covid 19 lockdown social program, brainchild of Northside Community Forum Ltd., whereby older community members were matched with younger volunteer 'Pen Pals' to ease the tedium of the lockdown years.

My Pen Pal, Dr Karen Hawke, who had worked as an epidemiologist associated with Australia's HIV/AIDS epidemic, was enthusiastic to see *I Don't Want to Talk About It* published and became my supportive co-participant in the ensuing Fox News US video, ABC Sydney radio programs, and ABC's *7.30 Report*, all produced under the directorship of Abby Edwards and featuring Tony's story as a significant part of our Pen Pals friendship.

Thank you dear Karen, and Abby.

Passionate that Tony's story be told, his siblings, Phil Carden, Carolyn Carden (Lynna) and Jane Mcnab, have shared its journey from its inception, contributing their reflections and their memories, proof-reading, and encouraging a sometimes dispirited writer . . .

Throughout the final stretch Jane has not only maintained the momentum until *I Don't Want to Talk About It* reached its finishing post but she has also been my backstop, particularly with technical issues, throughout the publishing process and the publicity program. Thank you and my gratitude always, dear Jane, Phil and Lynna.

About the Author

Lesley Saddington has garnered a wealth of experience through a range of employment, including voluntary vocations. For several years she worked as a medical technologist at Sydney Hospital's Kanematsu Institute of Pathology and in more recent times has taught entomology and horticulture at the Ryde College of TAFE. In 2002, she was made a Senior Fellow of the Australian Institute of Horticulture for her contribution to Australian horticulture.

She holds qualifications in medical technology, entomology, horticulture, landscape design, viticulture and arboriculture.

Following the death of her son, Tony Carden, from AIDS in 1995, Lesley trained to become an Ankali volunteer (Ankali is the Koori word for 'friend'). For eight years she provided Ankali support to four people following their diagnosis with HIV/AIDS and supported them throughout the duration of their illnesses.

Lesley is widowed, has three adult children and eight grandchildren and lives on the South Coast of New South Wales. She enjoys playing music (piano, cornet and recorder), gardening and growing exotic orchids.

www.ingramcontent.com/pod-product-compliance
Lightning Source LLC
Chambersburg PA
CBHW030033100526
44590CB00011B/191